Landscape with
Canals

Landscape with Canals

The Second Part of his Autobiography

L.T.C. ROLT

SUTTON PUBLISHING

First published in the United Kingdom in 1977

First published in this edition in 1984 by
Alan Sutton Publishing Limited, an imprint of
Sutton Publishing Limited
Phoenix Mill · Thrupp · Stroud · Gloucestershire GL5 2BU

Reprinted 1986, 1994, 1995, 1998

A catalogue record for this book is available from the British Library

Cover picture: detail from a painting by Felix Kelly

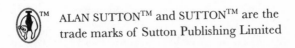 ALAN SUTTON™ and SUTTON™ are the
trade marks of Sutton Publishing Limited

Typesetting and origination by
Sutton Publishing Limited.
Printed in Great Britain by
WBC Limited, Bridgend, Mid-Glamorgan.

Contents

		page
1	An Interrupted Honeymoon	13
2	From Berkshire to Worcestershire	25
3	Eighteen Hundred Days in Tardebigge	44
4	Getting into Print	69
5	Canal Crusade	91
6	Sharpness and the Northern Canals	121
7	Pont Cysyllte – An Ambition Achieved	144
8	The End of the Cut	166

List of Illustrations

1. Kegworth Top Lock, River Soar, August 1939
2. On a lock gate, Kennet & Avon Canal, early 1930s
3. Wartime mooring at Tardebigge, 1941–6
4. Harry Rogers of Ironbridge
5. The Worcester & Birmingham Canal empty and under repair, late 1940s
6. Cressy at Lifford bridge, Stratford Canal
7. Lifford bridge
8. Cressy at King's Norton Stop Lock
9. Crossing Pont Cysyllte, 1949
10. Mooring at Vron Cysyllte
11. Duke's Cut, July 1950.
12. Sonia Smith on Warwick on the Grand Union Canal, 1950
13. The author steering Cressy at Hawkesbury Stop, 1950

Acknowledgements

Thanks are due to the following for granting reproduction permission: Mary Finelli for No. 2, Eric de Maré for Nos 3 and 5; the Estate of Angela Rolt for Nos 4, 9 and 11; *Illustrated London News* for Nos 6, 7 and 8. The other illustrations are from the author's collection.

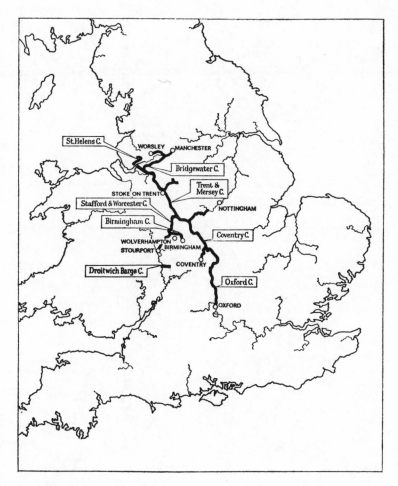

The first canals

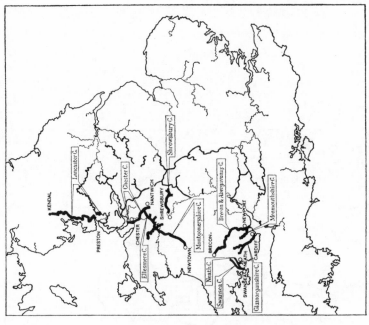

The waterways of the west

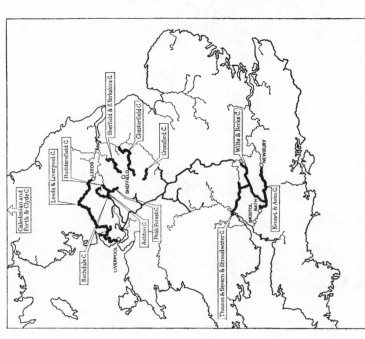

The coast to coast routes

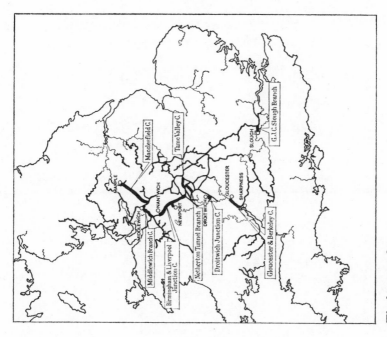

The last canals

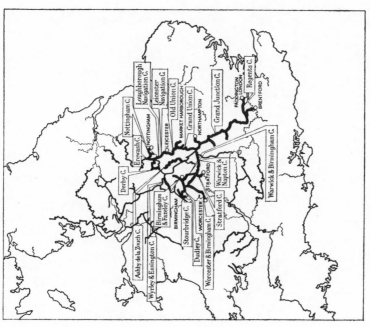

The Midlands network

Chapter 1

An Interrupted Honeymoon

August is not the best month to choose for a honeymoon, especially as the year was 1939. Summer suddenly seemed to become over-blown. In the bleached fields, burdened trees stood motionless, their shapes of dark, lack-lustre green resembling those of the threatening cumulus clouds whose heavy froth hung high in the still air above them. The atmosphere was stagnant and oppressive; days had a sullen, brooding quality and the breathless nights, lit only by the flicker of summer lightning, brought no relief. Our minds became curiously disturbed so that we longed for something that would break an almost unbearable tension. Small wonder that it should be a season when accidents and great disasters happen and when wars break out.

Yet a design for living so long dreamed about and finally achieved after so many difficulties was not to be abandoned, no matter how threatening the portents might seem. Angela and I had married in July, and the beginning of August found us heading north up the Leicester section of the Grand Union Canal in our new floating home, the narrow boat *Cressy*. Our ultimate objective, we hoped, was Llangollen, for I planned to fulfil a long cherished ambition by piloting *Cressy* over Telford's great aqueduct of Pont Cysyllte.

It would be wrong to convey the impression that we did not enjoy ourselves, but our happiness was far from unalloyed and my memories of this first voyage are bitter-sweet. The implacable hostility of Angela's father towards our marriage and the growing menace of war were two subjects we never discussed but could not forget. Never to be dispelled, they seemed to

13

hang always, like those thunderclouds, on the horizon of consciousness.

The inland waterways of England are a little world of their own, a world which, in 1939, was but little known and still possessed its own indigenous population of working boatmen and their families, many of whom we had come to know and to admire. It had seemed to us that these narrow waters possessed some magic power to insulate both them and us from the feverish and fretful hurly-burly of the larger world around us. It was this feeling of detachment, so hard to define, which had drawn me to them in the first place and had made the idea of living on a canal boat so attractive for one who aspired to become a writer. But, on this first voyage, the world we had known proved hard to forget or forsake. Disturbing news kept breaking in. As we lay at moorings on the river Soar below Leicester we heard on the radio the news that W. B. Yeats, the poet who, above all others, I most admired, had died at Cap Martin. I could hardly bring myself to believe that he was dead. The very next day we bought a local paper in the village shop at Barrow-on-Soar and read that Sir John Bowen, a recent ex-boy-friend of Angela's who had taken our marriage very hard, had crashed his Maserati during a motor race at Donnington Park and had been killed instantly. Angela was deeply shocked and we both felt in some degree responsible for his death. The news of these two wholly unconnected events added to the growing sense of insecurity and fatality during that doom-laden month. Life had never seemed so disturbingly ephemeral.

It was as we were travelling up the Trent & Mersey Canal towards Burton that the sultry weather broke. Dark thunderclouds rolled steadily up the sky astern, birds ceased their singing and the evening became very still and tense as distant thunder growled and muttered over the Trent valley. We moored up hurriedly near the village of Findern about six o'clock as the first heavy rain drops began to pock the water. The storm raged for over four hours, the roar of the rain on our roof so loud that it almost drowned the crashes of thunder. Yet all this fury seemed to bring no release of tension, for the next morning was overcast and still sultry.

We were approaching Stoke-on-Trent and had stopped to
take on some fuel at Trentham Bridge when the boatman at the
tiller of an oncoming horse-boat gave us the news that Hitler
had invaded Poland. War now seemed to be inevitable, but so
long as the slenderest hope remained we could only go forward.
That day we passed through the heart of the Potteries, through
the pandemonium of the Shelton steelworks and so through the
long darkness of the summit tunnel at Harecastle into Cheshire.
We moored that night near a canal-side pub called the 'Red
Bull' at Lawton and when, after dinner, we went along the
towpath for a drink we were surprised to find it in darkness. It
was our first experience of the black-out. Two days later we
had descended the long flight of locks which leads down from
the summit into the Cheshire Plain and were approaching
Middlewich when we heard on our radio the solemn voice of
Neville Chamberlain announce that Britain had declared war on
Germany.

Now the worst that we had feared had happened, what next?
After only a few brief weeks, all our hopes and carefully laid
plans seemed to lie in ruins. A great question mark hung over
our future. Angela burst into tears. I tried to console her by
saying that the outbreak of war was not our personal mis-
fortune but involved everyone in similarly agonizing situations,
but this was cold comfort. She insisted that our situation was
different and she foresaw a bleak future in which either *Cressy*
would have to be abandoned or she would be left living alone on
the boat, friendless in a strange district.

Our first reaction to such disastrous news as this was to
assume that it would immediately cause the whole fabric of life
to disintegrate; that every able-bodied man would instantly be
called up; that all fuel supplies would dry up forthwith leaving
the roads choked with useless cars; that trains would cease to
run and even clocks might cease to tell the time as they did
before. In fact we were to learn that even in the direst national
emergency there is a certain inevitability of gradualness about
the way our lives are changed by it. It is the sudden recognition
that change must come, rather than change itself, which pro-
duces the initial shock. We spent most of the rest of that
day somewhat miserably trying to adjust ourselves to a new

situation and making plans to meet it. It was obvious that our original objective of Llangollen would have to be abandoned. It was equally obvious – though this was a bitter disappointment to me – that my ambition to become a writer which was part and parcel of our new life must also be abandoned and that I must return to engineering. War had no use for a putative writer, I argued, but every use for an engineer, particularly one who could move house so readily. But how could I remain mobile? Petrol rationing would surely come, and of petrol *Cressy*'s engine consumed a gallon every three miles. Already we had travelled 190 miles from our base at Banbury. The only solution to this seemed to be to convert her Ford engine to burn paraffin, remaining moored in Cheshire until the necessary parts arrived. Meanwhile, where in the neighbourhood was I most likely to get myself a job? No sooner had I asked myself this question than I had the answer pat – at the Rolls Royce works at Crewe, where the famous twelve-cylinder Merlin engine which powered the Spitfire and the Hurricane was in production.

So we sailed on from Middlewich to Nantwich, whence I travelled by bus to the Rolls Royce works. As luck would have it, I had found among the few personal documents I had brought to the boat – little thinking I would so soon need them – the 'papers' which proved that I had served my five years' apprenticeship in the shops and testified to my experience and ability. After carefully scrutinizing these and asking me some searching questions, my interviewer at Rolls Royce told me I could start work as a fitter on the following Monday morning, but that I would have to join the Amalgamated Engineering Union. This was my first experience of a 'closed shop'. Instinctively I reacted against such coercion, but I had no option but to comply; and so, for the first and only time in my life, I became the holder of a Union card.

We had thought that the canal basin at Nantwich would be a strategically suitable mooring but we found that, try as we would, we could not get *Cressy* into it. The basin was disused commercially and the traffic on the main line of the Shropshire Union Canal, which at that time was quite considerable, had thrown up an impenetrable bar of mud across the entrance. So we had tied up at an inconvenient mooring out on the main line and now debated what we should do, poring over our ordnance map of the district. On our journey from Middlewich we had passed close by the little village of Church Minshull and had thought how attractive it looked. Now we saw from the map that it was only a short distance by by-roads from the Rolls Royce works. The only snag was that there was no bus service. We should have to be self-sufficient so far as transport was concerned. So I went into Nantwich, where I bought a second-hand bicycle for Angela and for myself an old square tank 2¾ h.p. A.J.S. motorcycle for a total outlay of £10. We laid the bicycle on the cabin top and I made a crude wooden cradle which supported the A.J.S. upright on the aft deck. Then, with our road transport safely stowed on board, we 'winded' *Cressy* with difficulty, turning her in the muddy mouth of the basin, and set off back to Church Minshull.

It was over eight years since I had last worked for a large engineering firm and although I realized that changes must have taken place during that time, I assumed that my new job would prove rewarding, so much did I revere the name of Rolls Royce. To me, it was synonymous with engineering craftsman-ship. Remembering how I had built diesel engines during my time at R. A. Listers of Dursley, I now imagined myself fitting up Merlin engines from scratch in the same way, afterwards accompanying them to the test bed to ensure that they per-formed satisfactorily. I was to be sadly disillusioned when I left Church Minshull for Crewe on my elderly motorcycle early on the following Monday morning.

No daylight ever penetrated the big shop. For twenty-four hours a day, mercury vapour lamps blazed overhead. I had never encountered this type of lighting before. It made all my new workmates look as if they were suffering from serious heart or liver complaints; their complexions looked ghastly and their lips were blue. They were working a night-shift at Rolls Royce. Walking from the light and fresh air of an autumn morning into the unnatural glare of this shop, its atmosphere used to hit me like a blow in the face. Warm and stale, it reeked of a nauseating mixture of suds, stale cigarette smoke and sweaty, unwashed humanity. Instead of assembling engines as I had fondly imagined, I found myself tapping the holes for the cylinder-head studs in an endless succession of Merlin cylinder blocks which appeared before me. A jig was first clamped to the block through which the long shank of the tap passed, thus making it impossible to tap the holes crooked and so removing the last vestige of human skill from the work. It struck me as a job which an ape might have been trained to perform, and I reflected wryly on the care with which my credentials had been scrutinized and on the fact that I had been compelled to join a so-called 'craft union' before being assigned this mindless task. Nowadays, such a row of holes would be both drilled and tapped under a giant multi-spindle machine. In fact my monotonous task represented only a brief transitional stage in the process of 'building the skill into the tool', but to me it was a new and disturbing phenomenon. I despair of conveying the depths of boredom and apathy to which this job rapidly reduced me. I even found myself looking forward eagerly to my next visit to the urinal because it relieved the tedium. After such an experience, the strikes that have plagued the engineering industry since the war are no surprise to me. No amount of money can make such durance any less vile.

The contrast between my daytime occupation and the life of the canals to which I returned each evening at dusk was extreme. Then I would see *Cressy*, lying beside the graceful arc of the humped canal bridge, a long dark shape with chinks of golden light showing here and there through gaps in our improvised black-out arrangements. Once I had gained the refuge of this small island of warmth and stillness where the bindings of familiar books glowed in the mellow lamplight, my working days seemed like some bad dream. Not a nightmare exactly, but one of those disquieting dreams which continue to recur despite intervals of wakefulness. What made things so much worse was that we could foresee no end to it; no light at the end of the tunnel; the future could only grow darker.

But deliverance from this bondage arrived unexpectedly in the shape of a letter from my old employer at the village foundry at Aldbourne in Wiltshire where I had last worked in 1933. It had been forwarded to me by my parents. Owing to the wartime 'grow more food' campaign which was then just getting under way, his small business was extremely busy and he was desperately short-handed. Could I come down and help him out? The weekly wage he offered was less than half what I was getting at Rolls Royce, but the answer was an unhesitating Yes. So, after six weeks which had felt like six months, I 'asked for my cards' at Rolls Royce, keeping my Union card and my little RR lapel badge as souvenirs.

Meanwhile, the paraffin vaporizer I had ordered for *Cressy's* Model T Ford engine had arrived and it was a simple matter to fit it in place of the existing water-cooled manifold. Opposite the petrol tank against the aft-bulkhead there was already a twenty-five-gallon paraffin tank in which we stored fuel for lamps and stoves, so it was easy to run a second fuel line from this to the carburettor. We would still need a small amount of petrol for starting and warming up, but apart from this we should now be able to snap our fingers at petrol rationing. Normally, to keep *Cressy* at her stately cruising gait of 3 m.p.h., her engine ran at little more than a fast idling speed, and my one doubt was whether this would be sufficient to keep the manifold hot enough to vaporize the fuel.

We had to make a preliminary trip to Middlewich in order to 'wind' *Cressy* at the junction with the Trent & Mersey Canal below Wardle Lock, for I did not intend to head south by the roundabout route by which we had come. The engine ran perfectly on its new fuel; the exhaust was remarkably clean and a check showed that there was no dilution of the sump oil. In fact, it never gave any trouble throughout the lifetime of the boat, the only minor disadvantage being that, unless I turned over to petrol, the engine had to be kept running in locks.

On 15 November, with the bicycle and the A.J.S. on board, we set sail from Church Minshull, our ultimate destination being Hungerford on the Kennet & Avon Canal. Having served its immediate purpose we were in two minds whether or not to leave the motorcycle behind, but in the event it proved unexpectedly useful as a tender. For example, when we moored for the night at Norbury Junction on the Shropshire Union main line, I unshipped it and rode into Newport to do the week-end's shopping with Angela behind me on the pillion.

That late autumn voyage was wholly pleasurable. The weather was unusually fine for the time of the year, the tension and oppression we had both felt in August seemed to have vanished, and for my part I was delighted to be free once more after my brief spell of servitude. After long days spent at the tiller in the fresh air of autumn, how satisfying it was to tie up in some remote place, to go below, shut the hatches and settle down with a book in an easy chair beside the glowing fire. It was at such times that one savoured most keenly the contrast between the warmth and comfort of our cabin and the silence, the darkness and the loneliness of the world outside. For the long level pounds of the Shropshire Union command a great expanse of open country which rolls away westward to the distant Wrekin; even after darkness had fallen I remained very conscious of this landscape, so clearly was it registered by the mind's eye as the night wind stirred *Cressy* and set her bow nudging the bank.

The first week of December saw us back on the Oxford canal. Winter had set in early and on the last stage of her journey from Cropredy to Banbury, *Cressy* had to cleave a path for herself through the ice which had formed on the canal overnight. I planned to stay at Tooley's Boatyard at Banbury over Christmas while minor repairs were done to our boat; for we should be mooring for an indefinite period on a disused canal where there would be no repair facilities and where we should be far from any dry dock. But our stay at Banbury proved to be far more protracted than I expected. That first winter of the war was hard and bitter. For two months we lay locked fast in ice too thick for any ice-breaker boat to conquer and it was not until 1 March 1940 that we were able to slip our moorings and head south for Oxford and the Thames.

Cressy had never navigated the Thames before and neither had I. Due to the sudden thaw, we found the river was running fast and high, so that it was not without some apprehension that we locked out on to it through Isis Lock at Oxford. In time of flood, one always feels safer in a large and heavy boat when travelling upstream, for however slow one's progress may be as the boat battles against the current, at least it is fully under control because it always has steerage way. In order to maintain steerage way going downstream, however, the boat has to travel at a speed faster than the current. This meant that *Cressy* was soon sweeping down the Thames at a speed of 6 m.p.h. or more which, compared with her stately pace on the canals, seemed a positively dizzy velocity. It was also as alarming a sensation as driving a car without any brakes because I knew that even by putting her hard astern I could not hope to stop her. Fortunately, there were sufficient stretches of slack water at the heads of the lock cuts to enable me to get way off her in time to avoid crashing into the lock gates.

Our first 'moment' came at Abingdon that evening. We asked the lock keeper at Abingdon Lock if he knew of a suitable place to moor and he gave us singularly bad advice by suggesting a small pleasure garden just above Abingdon bridge. I put *Cressy* full astern and held her bow into the bank so that Angela could jump ashore with a line and make it fast to a convenient tree. But we realized too late that the current at this point was running like a mill race. The cotton line parted with a crack like a pistol shot, and *Cressy* swung across the stream until she was in imminent danger of crashing broadside into the piers of the bridge just below. Instantly I threw the reversing lever from full astern to full ahead, swung the rudder over and, a moment later, had shot safely through the arch to find myself sailing swiftly past the old waterfront of Abingdon, leaving Angela stranded on the bank. I doubted whether I would be able to stop the boat single-handed before reaching Culham Lock cut, but fortunately I spotted an individual who looked like a waterman standing on a little jetty close beside the river. I shouted to him, threw him my stern line which he deftly caught, and between us we managed to bring *Cressy* in to the bank. Presently, Angela appeared, walking down the opposite bank of the river, and was ferried across by an obliging boatman. The moral of this little incident should be obvious to any tyro, but it had not appeared obvious to us I am ashamed to say. It is that when a heavy boat is moving with the current it should always be checked with the stern line and not by the bow.

Another alarming incident occurred next morning as we were sailing rapidly down the broad reach between Wallingford and Cleeve Lock. I suddenly saw to my horror a stout cable, secured to a stake on either bank, lying across the river. As it was almost awash, it had remained invisible until the last moment. *Cressy* stretched that cable like an arrow in a taut bowstring. Then both the stakes tore out of the ground, the cable sank and we floated over safely as I had meanwhile stopped our propeller. Later, when we complained bitterly to the lock keeper at Cleeve about this lethal obstruction, he explained that a Canadian contingent of the Royal Engineers had been practising building pontoon bridges and had obviously gone away without removing their cable. He promised to pass on our complaint to their C.O. It was the first war-time hazard we had encountered.

We reached Reading without any further incident and moored above Blake's Lock on the river Kennet just after noon on 6 March. Ahead of us lay the most difficult part of our long journey, a waterway disused and virtually derelict. The first eighteen miles of it to Newbury was the old Kennet Navigation, built in 1723 and consisting partly of the river Kennet and partly of artificial cuts. For the last lap of our journey, from Newbury to Hungerford, we should be on the Kennet & Avon Canal proper.

The Kennet, like the Thames, was running high, but now we were travelling upstream and there were times when we were only just able to make headway against the current with our engine flat out. Altogether, in those last $27\frac{1}{2}$ miles to Hungerford I think we must have encountered every kind of hazard known to the inland navigator. In the first place, the reach of the Kennet through Reading between Blake's and County Locks was tricky in the extreme. Not only was the river very narrow and tortuous and the current swift, but to make matters worse, the brick walls of buildings rose sheer from the water on either side creating a kind of miniature man-made Grand Canyon. When we had ploughed our way up to County Lock, suffering no more than the odd bump or two, I asked the lock keeper there how on earth horse-drawn boats ever succeeded in making such a passage. 'Oh,' he replied. 'They used to float a long line down to 'em, see.' This is the kind of facile answer which one accepts at the time only to puzzle over later. It could not have been quite as easy as that. And how about travelling downstream? Did they just surrender themselves to the mercy of the current?

Armed with an extra long windlass for raising the rusty lock paddles, we headed for Newbury. I salute the memory of the bygone boatmen of the Kennet & Avon, for the Kennet Navigation might have been deliberately laid out to create the maximum amount of difficulty for the navigator. The downstream entrances to the lock cuts were so positioned that the river would very soon deposit a bar of silt across their mouths. And because most of the locks were sited at the head of these cuts instead of near their tails where they should have been, there was no hope of scouring these shoals away with a flush from the lower gate paddles. We just had to haul over them as best we could. From Burghfield onwards most of the lock chambers were the originals of 1723 with sloping turf sides instead of masonry walls. Guard rails, made from old G.W.R. broad gauge bridge rails, had been installed to prevent boats from settling on to these sloping sides, but this meant that it was very difficult to get on to or off the boat once it was in a chamber. These old locks must have been very slow to fill at the best of times, but now filling had become practically impossible because the amount of water leaking out through the rotten lower gates almost equalled that coming in through the top gate paddles. Fortunately there were plenty of reeds about. We gathered armfuls of them, sinking these bundles in the locks with our long shaft till they had staunched the worst of the leaks in the gates.

The many swing bridges across the waterway caused us even more difficulty than the locks. Some of these carried motor roads and, to prevent heavy traffic damaging the cast-iron ball bearings on which they swung, the left- and right-hand threaded buckles of their bracing rods had been slacked right off until the bridge deck rested solid on its brick abutments. In such cases, the bridge-swinging operation began with the tedious preliminary of tightening up these buckles with a tommy bar. Even when this had been done, however, our troubles were not over, for when the roadway had been resurfaced no attempt had been made to prevent the tarred chippings from fouling the slots between the bridge and its abutments. With half the able-bodied males of the village heaving on crow-bars under the direction of the red-faced landlord of the 'Row Barge' and with *Cressy* going full astern, her bow line fast to a bridge railing post, it took us three hours to open the bridge at Woolhampton.

However, all these obstacles were eventually overcome and at four o'clock on 12 March we tied up at the far end of Wooldridge's Wharf, just below the tail of Hungerford Lock and within striking distance of the foundry at Aldbourne. This pleasant, secluded and convenient mooring in crystal clear water was to be our home for just over twelve months. Beside our boat was an old weather-boarded shed with a tiled roof which contained a saw-pit. Assuming it to be disused, we made use of it as a convenient store shed. But to our surprise, on one occasion not long after we arrived, two men appeared, took the long pitsaw down from its hooks under the rafters, and proceeded to saw a log of timber into planks. Although we watched this operation with fascinated interest, we had no conception then that we were witnessing a spectacle that neither we nor, I suspect, anyone else would ever see again in England. For the last two wars changed all our lives, sweeping away into the limbo of memory a wealth of custom and traditional usages. This is why these wars appear to create rapids in the steady stream of time of a velocity out of all proportion to their actual duration. This has made the time we moored at Hungerford now seem an infinitely remote happening in a bygone age, and the scene of the two sawyers wielding their great saw as poignantly archaic as some medieval illumination.

Chapter 2

From Berkshire to Worcestershire

Before we left Banbury on our honeymoon cruise I had already decided on the subject for my first book – it would be the story of our voyage through the canals. Although I did no writing during the first weeks, with this book in mind I kept a very full log of each day's journey including details of our excursions ashore. All further thought of this project had been laid aside when I took the job at Rolls Royce, but as soon as we decided to move south my sense of relief was such that I took it up again eagerly. Besides keeping my log as fully as ever, I began writing the book itself during the long autumn evenings, sitting at the desk I had built in *Cressy*'s cabin. The great spell of frost which immobilized us at Banbury had provided a heaven-sent opportunity for writing, with the result that by the time the thaw came and we could leave Banbury I had completed all but the last chapter or so. I finished it a few weeks after our arrival in Hungerford. There then began that deflating and depressing experience that is the common lot of aspiring authors. Over the next few months my precious manuscript, which I had entitled *A Painted Ship* from the well-known line in *The Ancient Mariner*, must have visited practically every publisher in London. It bounced back with unfailing regularity, sometimes with a polite note, but more usually with a printed rejection slip. Only two publishers, both with famous names, showed a flicker of interest. One undertook to publish the book at my expense, while the other offered me £75 outright for it. So poor was I at this time that the latter offer tempted me sorely, but I had read somewhere some cautionary words warning the tyro against the wicked ways of publishers and, very fortunately, refused. Had it not been for the war which had driven me back into engineering and thus given me another source of livelihood, I might well have accepted the tempting bait of that £75 down for the sake of getting my name into print. So, what may seem a disaster at the time can turn out to be for the best in the long run.

My final fling was to send my manuscript to that well-known literary agent, A. D. Peters. He returned it with a curt note declining to handle it. It was at this point that I gave up in bitter disappointment. For I argued that whereas a publisher's refusal was understandable because he had to back his faith in a book with hard cash, refusal on the part of an agent, who had nothing to lose and only his commission to gain, amounted to sentence of death. Sorrowfully, I put my literary creation back on the shelf and tried to forget about it. Those publishers who had troubled to reply had given as their reason for rejection the fact that, in their judgement, there was insufficient public interest in the subject of canals. Were they right, or was this their way of being tactful? Perhaps I should never find out.

Of my work at Aldbourne and of the foundry I need say little because I have already described my earlier experience there in the first volume of this autobiography, and now I found that there had been little change. The job was as varied and as interesting as it had been before, work in the little shop alternating with excursions to downland farms to deal with some ailing tractor, stationary engine or farm implement. Scarcely a day passed that did not bring some fresh challenge to one's ingenuity and skill, so that I could not help reflecting wryly that for this work I received half as much as I had earned in my mindless job at Rolls Royce. I realized then that wages were no longer related to skill but had become a form of compensation for its forfeiture and for all the drudgery and the wanton waste of life and talent which such deprivation involves. So I did not begrudge my meagre wage; it seemed a small price to pay for my release from bondage.

One thing I found saddening was that I no longer had old Mark Palmer as a work-mate. That rare character had now retired and was living in the village on his old age pension. Wearing a new trilby hat and a gabardine and looking unnaturally clean and tidy, he would often come pottering up the village street for a yarn with us. He must have wasted quite a lot of our time, but in a country workshop such interruptions are tolerated and no one ever questioned his right as an old and valued craftsman to come and go as he wished. Mark's eyes still twinkled with life behind his spectacles, and his tales were as richly humorous as ever.

As a result of the war, the downland landscape was beginning to change. For the first time in living memory its sheep-walks were coming under the plough. Already slopes that had seemed immemorially green were chequered with squares of brown arable, some already misted with the green of winter wheat, others bare and ready for the drill. It was the beginning of a transformation that would soon leave only a few of the steepest slopes untilled. I viewed this change with mixed feelings. After the agricultural depression and consequent rural dilapidation and neglect, any renewal of activity seemed welcome. On the other hand, the frantic speed with which this primeval landscape was being transformed into a huge mechanized ranch farm, ruthlessly exploiting its stored fertility, sickened and saddened me. It represented no change of heart towards the land, only a desperate reaction to an emergency. White patches like melting snow on the new-ploughed slopes revealed how desperately thin was the precious flesh of top-soil upon the bare bones of the chalk.

It was obvious that there was going to be the heaviest corn harvest that Wiltshire had ever known, and it was this prospect that had prompted the signal for help which had reached me in Cheshire. The combine harvester was as yet virtually unknown in England and the tool which would harvest this Wiltshire wheat crop was the power-driven reaper and binder, a machine driven, not by its landwheel as on the old horse-drawn binders, but by the tractor's power take-off. In May of 1940 I was instructed to go to Trafford Park where, I was told, the firm of Massey Harris had set up a 'binder school' for the instruction of those who would have to service their latest machines. So Angela and I drove northwards in an elderly 'chummy' Austin

27

Seven which I had borrowed and, on arrival, found lodgings in a depressing, blackened street on the outskirts of Manchester.

I soon discovered that the so-called 'binder school' was no more than a device for attracting a supply of cheap labour. For its pupils were immediately set to work assembling new machines from components which had arrived in crates from America via the Manchester Ship Canal. The one intricate portion of the machine about which I had hoped to learn more was the knotter mechanism which tied up each sheaf with binder twine. But as this device emerged from the crate in the form of a complete assembly which we merely had to bolt in its appropriate place, I was left none the wiser. In any case, our sojourn at Trafford Park was destined to be much briefer than I had supposed. For the months of 'the phoney war' were over; this was the time of the fall of France and the rescue of the British army from Dunkirk by the 'little ships'. No one knew what would happen next; there were rumours of invasion and, fearing that we might become stranded in the north, my employer sent a telegram bidding me return to Aldbourne immediately. So we headed south again, I knowing no more about power-driven binders than I had done when we set out.

Nevertheless, I found myself regarded from then on as the local binder expert, a wholly unmerited reputation I found hard to uphold when harvest time came round and I was sent out in answer to distress calls from farmers whose machines had gone wrong in the field. As I had feared, it was usually that infernal mechanism, the knotter, which gave trouble. Crudely executed yet as complex as a knitting machine, it was subject to subtle derangements that caused it to play the most infuriating tricks. Sometimes it seemed to suffer from constipation, finally ejecting with difficulty the most enormous sheaf. Sometimes the opposite would take place and it would proffer a pitiful bundle of four or five corn stalks loosely bound together with twine. At others, it would seemingly tire altogether of the task of endlessly tying knots and eject the sheaves unbound, carelessly throwing a short piece of twine after each one as though to say, 'Here, you do it for a change.' However, by a mixture of low cunning and perseverance I usually managed to get the better of this mechanical monstrosity in the end and so preserve my bogus reputation.

We had returned from Trafford Park to find unwonted activity on the Kennet & Avon Canal. In the War Office, some brass-hat who had probably never seen the canal in his life must have spotted its course from the Thames to the Bristol Avon on a map and decided that it was a ready-made defence line. So the old canal had emerged from nearly a century of neglect and obscurity to become the 'Blue Defence Line', an object of national strategic importance. Even at this most critical period of the war when we expected at any moment to hear the sound of church bells signalling Nazi invasion, there was something irresistibly comic about this decision and the action which followed it. In the light of our recent experience, one imagined villagers armed with crow-bars struggling to open the old wooden swing bridges in the face of advancing Panzer Divisions. In any event, the canal was no more than waist-deep in many places.

Now, concrete pill-boxes were built beside each lock, and since many of these sites were inaccessible by road, being islanded between river and canal, this was a work of considerable difficulty. In this emergency, one very old man, reputedly the last of the Kennet & Avon boatmen, who had been living in a ramshackle houseboat below Colthrop Mills, was dragged out of retirement and put in charge of a leaking maintenance boat which must have been nearly as old as himself. A broken-down horse, led by a dim-witted youth, provided the traction. Tipping lorries laden with aggregate roared on to Wooldridge's Wharf, depositing their burdens at the waterside for conveyance by water to Hungerford Marsh Lock. So we had the unique experience of seeing a working horse-boat on the Kennet & Avon. It did not last long, however. The weather was hot and the old boatman and his mate evidently found it thirsty work. Returning from a trip to Hungerford Marsh one evening, they tied up their empty boat at the wharf and adjourned to the pub opposite. Meanwhile, the men on the wharf, inspired by a greater sense of the urgency of the operation, proceeded to overload the boat before going home. By the time the crew returned from their protracted drinking session, only the diminutive cabin of their boat was still showing above water. Thus the Kennet & Avon's contribution to the war effort came to a premature end and how the remaining pill-boxes were completed remains a mystery.

When the contractors reached the summit level of the canal at Savernake, they were dismayed to see their Blue Defence Line disappearing underground. Not to be outdone, they dug a small ditch over the top of the tunnel. One feels it was providential that information about Britain's ground defences never penetrated to Hitler, otherwise he would surely have ordered his invasion fleet to sail forthwith. As it was, he inexplicably resorted to air attack with results that made history.

During those weeks of the Battle of Britain the whole bowl of the night sky reverberated like some huge deep-toned gong as the bomber fleets of the Luftwaffe passed high overhead en route for the industrial Midlands and then returned again having laid their deadly eggs. To our surprise the lady on the wharf from whom we obtained our milk complained bitterly of lack of sleep. In response to our solicitous inquiries she explained that nights spent under her kitchen table were the cause of her insomnia. Nor was she by any means the only one, we discovered, to adopt this ostrich-like policy, a fact which led us to conclude that our instinct for self-preservation must be underdeveloped. One night, indeed, *Cressy* shuddered from stem to stern as a stick of bombs fell nearby. The momentary glare from the open fire-door of a passing goods train on the nearby railway had attracted the attention of a stray bomber, but fortunately his load fell harmlessly, straddling the railway embankment immediately to the west of the little town. So far as I know, these were the only bombs to fall in the district.

Nevertheless, the Blitz had its effect on Hungerford. The town became a reception area for 'evacuees' from the East End of London, with disturbing results for all concerned. Respectable country folk could find no common ground with gaunt, loud-mouthed, feckless women whose domestic economy had been based on street-corner pubs and chip shops, while hordes of ragged children, many of them verminous, who did not even know that milk came from cows, provoked reactions of shock and horror. This was not simply a case of the rich and washed reacting against a sudden invasion of the poor and unwashed, as socialist theorists proclaimed at the time. For, as my own case proved, the level of wages in the country was far lower than in the big towns. For those who could read the lesson of this unexpected confrontation aright it revealed only too clearly the evils of industrialism: the degradation, the loss of responsibility and self-respect, the complete alienation from the natural world that it brought about. Of this state of affairs I had first been made forcibly aware fifteen years earlier by the annual invasion of the farm at Pitchill by 'the Dudleys' from the Black Country. Obviously there had since been no change for the better.

It was not only to East Enders that Hungerford gave refuge. Some old friends of mine who owned a small hotel in the High Street gave asylum to the paintings of a London art collector. It was an unusual and unrepeatable experience to sit drinking beer in the snug, contemplating works by Henri Matisse or Renoir instead of the more conventional, yellowed Cecil Aldin prints which they had temporarily displaced. Self-conscious art worship amid the distractions of a great public gallery can be no substitute for such peaceful and private acquaintance.

I now recognized a truth that should have become obvious to me long before. This was that for anyone who, like myself, possessed no inherited means or influence, it is impossible to lead a full life and at the same time to enjoy financial security. This may not always have been so, but in the modern world the two aims had become mutually exclusive. By relating them to 'higher productivity', wages had become a form of bribery – the more repetitive, monotonous and soul-destroying the work, the higher the wage – while in the upper echelons of the business world the single-minded pursuit of financial gain appeared to be the only secret of success. Between these upper and nether millstones of organized labour and big business, both wholly dedicated to the money in the till, the creative artist and craftsman seemed to me to be fated to be ground out of existence. Yet my own experience had convinced me that because the craftsman derived his satisfaction primarily from the work itself rather than from the reward it brought, he alone held the secret of the good life.

Nevertheless, money is something one cannot do without; and poverty, like the toothache, can play havoc with philosophers. Much as I was enjoying my work at Aldbourne, the harsh fact was that our finances were precarious in the extreme. All we had to supplement my slender weekly wage packet was the small allowance that Angela received, and such was her father's hostility towards us that we expected each month to find that he had cancelled this long-standing arrangement. These were the economic facts of life which persuaded me to abandon the foundry at Aldbourne and to become, of all things, a civil servant, albeit a temporary one.

The agent of this change was my old friend Harry Rose. From the day we left school together my friendship with Harry had been of that rare kind that is taken for granted by both sides and remains wholly unaffected by long absence. We never corresponded, yet, on the rare occasions when our paths happened to cross, our intimacy seemed to be easily and effortlessly re-established no matter how many months or even years might have elapsed since our last meeting. One of these rare occasions occurred in the spring of 1941 when I returned from work to find Harry comfortably ensconced on the boat, having introduced himself to Angela whom he had never met. I always took Harry's infrequent and unlikely appearances for granted, but presumably in this case he had learned of our whereabouts from my parents. Harry, who had served his engineering apprenticeship in the Trafford Park works of Metropolitan Vickers, was now, he told us, working for the Ministry of Supply in a Department known as TT3 which was concerned with the production of vehicle spares for the three services and for essential civilian use. It was at this time occupying temporary headquarters in Bromsgrove School, though it would soon move to Chilwell Ordnance Depot and finally to offices in nearby Nottingham where it remained for the duration. Why didn't I join him? he asked: it was an interesting job which entailed visiting engineering works all over the country, and the salary he mentioned was approximately three times my present wage. Despite this tempting bait of wealth that seemed to me beyond the dreams of avarice, the prospect at first thought appalled me. All my life I had been almost as allergic to bureaucrats as to policemen, so how could I now consent to become one without sacrificing all principle? But Harry explained to me that his Department was staffed entirely by engineers recruited from industry, men whose one concern it was to cut red tape rather than to spin it. In Ministry jargon, I would be a temporary civil servant, not on the establishment. This put the suggestion in a more favourable light, although what finally persuaded me to act upon it was the fact that – how, I do not know – Harry had already joined the Department. A more uncivil servant than he it would be difficult to imagine.

So, as a result of Harry Rose's visit, I shortly afterwards reported to Bromsgrove, where I was interviewed by an imposing individual in military uniform whose name I forget and was given the job. I was told to report for duty in ten days' time, which left us precious little breathing space in which to make our own arrangements. Because time was of importance, I at first thought of sailing to the Midlands by what was, on the map, the shortest water route: westwards through the Kennet & Avon Canal to Bath and Bristol and thence to Avonmouth and straight up the tidal Severn to Sharpness. In view of the state of dereliction into which the western part of the Kennet & Avon has now fallen, it is interesting to recall the argument then advanced by that canal's railway owners. They did not dispute my right of passage and, indeed, undertook to see me through, but they advised me that such a passage would be hazardous. The Luftwaffe were paying Avonmouth Docks some unwelcome attention at the time and I was warned that I might have to remain in that uncomfortable spot for some days awaiting suitable conditions of weather and tide for the passage up the estuary to Sharpness, itself a risky proceeding for a narrow boat. Apart from the possibility of being blown out of the water, this need to wait, perhaps for weeks, at Avonmouth put the idea out of court anyway. Even at that time it was hopelessly optimistic, and I strongly suspect that at the end of a week we should still have been battling our way through the mud towards Bath. Under the circumstances, this would have been an embarrassing predicament, so we decided to return by the way we had come with the familiar boatyard at Banbury as our first objective. Because it was within striking distance by road from the Midlands, I could make Banbury my temporary base while *Cressy* was docked for repairs, before we moved on to some mooring as yet undecided which would be more convenient for my field of operations.

Having with some difficulty 'winded' *Cressy* below Hungerford bridge on the previous evening, we left Wooldridge's Wharf, bound for Reading, on 28 April 1941. In one respect our passage was easier than before; all the old wooden swing bridges opened readily. This they had been made to do the better to dismay the advancing Aryan hordes. Nevertheless, this voyage down to Reading was not without its moments. The springs were up, as they say in the chalk country, and Kennet was flowing fast. I fear we anathematized the memory of John Hore who had engineered the navigation in 1724 and had presumably been responsible for siting his locks at the upstream instead of at the downstream end of his lock cuts. On our upward journey we had had to battle with shoals of mud and now we experienced the other consequence of this mistake. It is disconcerting for the steerer of a heavy craft, borne along by a swift current, on rounding a turn to be suddenly confronted with the choice between a weir on the one hand and a pair of closed lock gates on the other, the one inviting shipwreck and the other a violent collision. Ham Mills Lock, below Newbury, is a good example of this hazard and we soon came to the conclusion that the downstream navigation of the Kennet when a 'fresh' is running was no job for a tyro.

On the strength of his tales of derring-do on the high seas with which he had regaled us, we had shipped as crew as far as Reading an enthusiastic yachtsman whose acquaintance we had made at Hungerford. It soon became evident, however, that to him no perils on the sea could equal those of the Kennet and his presence therefore added not a little to our difficulties. On sighting any obstruction ahead he would ignore our pleas to jump ashore with a line, and take a stance on our foredeck with our long shaft outstretched before him like a lance in rest as though preparing to repel boarders. It required a practical demonstration to convince him of the futility of this exercise where such a heavy boat was concerned. *Cressy* was coming into a lock and, despite my shouted assurance that she was fully under control in the engine department, our friend assumed his customary threatening posture at the bow. So intent was he upon the lock gates ahead that he failed to notice that he was holding the shaft in such a position that it would inevitably be trapped between these gates and the for'ard bulkhead of the boat. Sure enough, the long shaft bowed beneath his arm, lifting him off his feet, and then broke with a resounding crack. We were not amused. However, despite this and other more or less alarming incidents, we succeeded in reaching Blake's Lock at Reading in three days as compared with our five days of hard slogging on the upward journey.

On the morning of May Day, I swung *Cressy* out on to the Thames and headed for Oxford. Navigating the Kennet against time had been a kind of aquatic obstacle race, and it felt very good to be out in broad clear waters once more. *Cressy* seemed to share our relief for she fairly galloped along, covering the forty miles to Oxford in two days with a night stop near Benson Lock. Thanks to this good progress we were able to tie up at Tooley's Boatyard at Banbury at midday on 6 May.

Before I could start my new job I needed a car and, because I had laid up my own 12/50 Alvis for the duration, my father, who had become too old and infirm to drive, agreed that I might borrow his. So I travelled home to Stanley Pontlarge by train to collect it, little knowing that this was the last time I would see him alive. Over the next four months that gallant old car must have covered a greater mileage than it had done in my father's hands in the previous four years. My Department was as yet ill-organized and under-staffed, with the result that I had to travel to places as far afield as Grantham, Chesterfield and Shrewsbury, seldom getting back to Banbury except at week-ends. The Alvis proved itself a good ambassador. It was not exactly the type of vehicle that engineers normally associate with 'the man from the Ministry' and on this account they were the more ready to be friendly and cooperative.

One day in June, Angela received the news by wire at Banbury that my father had had a stroke. She managed to get in touch with me through the Department and we drove over to Stanley Pontlarge immediately, but were too late. On our arrival, my mother, dry-eyed and apparently unmoved, told us simply that he was dead. Leaving Angela below with her, I went at once to the spare bedroom where they had laid him. It was a perfect midsummer evening and the late sunlight streamed in through the west window of this airy, white-walled room. From the garden there rose a chorus of birdsong and a recurrent shrill whistling as a bevy of swifts, hawking for flies, dived past the window in rapid, glancing flight. But inside, the room itself seemed strangely silent and still. A faint sickly-sweet smell hung in the air. I stood at the foot of the bed gazing down at my father. It was my first acquaintance with death. His complexion was yellow and ghastly, but the stroke had not distorted his features. He looked calm and peaceful enough, yet his face appeared shrunken because those who had laid him out had removed his false teeth. They had placed them on the table beside him along with his worn gold signet ring with its crest of a Wyvern and his gold watch which still ticked busily as its spring steadily released the stored energy put into it by his dead hands. Curiously enough I found the pathos of these few familiar objects, imperishable, yet now lying cold and forlorn, much more moving than the sight of the perishable body with which they had lately been so intimately connected. It was these things rather than the shell that lay on the bed that seemed to me to symbolize the chrysalis from which the spirit had so lately flown.

My father was in his seventy-sixth year. As I looked my last on him my feeling was not so much of grief as of remorse and self-reproach. I thought of the many times I had sided with my mother in family arguments; of the youthful intolerance with which I had so often cut short his interminable and oft-repeated stories; of his many enthusiasms which I had churlishly refused to share. And now it was too late to make amends. As though fearful of disturbing him, I closed the door noiselessly and tiptoed away.

As I had expected, my father left only an overdraft, raised on the security of the property, and a number of almost worthless rubber shares. I have an old-fashioned, almost medieval, dislike of usury, so in defiance of legal advice I sold the latter for what little they would fetch in order to pay off the former. At least the house would now be unencumbered and my mother would be able to go on living there, free of debt, on her own small income.

By the end of August, *Cressy* had been docked and refurbished so that we were free to move elsewhere. My Department was by now better organized and it was becoming clear that my work in the future would be increasingly confined to the area around Redditch, Birmingham and Wolverhampton. We were therefore concerned to find some place to moor which would be in pleasant country yet at the same time within easy striking distance of these industrial areas. After a great deal of pondering over ordnance maps we decided that Tardebigge on the Worcester & Birmingham Canal looked the most promising. Although neither of us had ever been there, we could not have made a better choice as things turned out.

In order to make this move, I took the week's leave that was due to me and on 30 August we cast off from Banbury, travelling north up the Oxford Canal as far as Napton Junction where we turned left on to the main line of the Grand Union Canal, heading for Warwick and Birmingham. We found the so-called 'new' wide locks on this canal by far the heaviest to work of any we had so far encountered. The gates seemed unnecessarily massive and the helical paddle gearing slow and tedious to operate. Nevertheless, the night of 1 September found us moored at the summit of the flight of twenty-one locks at Hatton which lift the canal out of the valley of the Avon at Warwick. The next morning, we continued through Shrewley Tunnel and along the Grand Union as far as Kingswood Junction.

At Kingswood, a short arm links the Grand Union with the Stratford-on-Avon Canal, the northern section of which runs directly to join the Worcester & Birmingham Canal at King's Norton. From the map it had seemed an obvious short cut, saving a number of miles and at the same time avoiding the necessity of passing through the centre of Birmingham. But it soon became evident that a route that had appeared obvious on paper was by no means so inviting in reality. For the Stratford Canal, like the Kennet & Avon, was then owned by the Great Western Railway Company and, like the latter, it was in a semi-derelict state. We had known that the canal at

Stratford was long disused, but for some reason we optimistically assumed that this northern section, being part of a through route, was still frequented by commercial traffic. We discovered just how wrong we were as we struggled up the flight of nineteen narrow locks at Lapworth. The short pounds between them were so densely packed with weed that *Cressy*'s propeller instantly became an ineffectual ball of green wool and we had to resort to bow-hauling. We speculated gloomily that if the eleven-mile level from the top of these locks to King's Norton was no better than this, we should either have to hire a horse or admit defeat and retire stern first down the locks. Greatly to our relief, however, the summit level appeared to be clear apart from a little duck-weed on the surface. There also proved to be quite a reasonable depth of water and we were able to travel another four miles before tying up for the night. For the greater part of its length, this long upper level of the Stratford lies in a cutting, its steep sides so thickly overgrown that occasionally the branches of leaning trees almost met over the ribbon of dark water. We had to bring the bicycle down from the deck and lower our stove chimney to prevent them being swept away. As we slid through this long tunnel of green shade, it was difficult to believe that we were so close to Birmingham, so remote from the world did it seem. From the look of it, the towpath appeared to be unfrequented even by the fishermen one usually encounters, particularly near large towns. Imagine then our surprise when, on entering King's Norton tunnel next morning, we saw lights glimmering in the darkness ahead. It was as eerie as discovering signs of activity in some long disused mine and it recalled legends of the 'knockers' or 'the old men'. It turned out to be a gang of maintenance men re-pointing the brickwork of the tunnel vault from a staging rigged on a maintenance boat, a sight which, though prosaic, was remarkable enough on a railway-owned canal. I think the gang were even more surprised to see us than we were to see them, and as we inched our way slowly past their boat in the gloom with precious little room to spare, our voices, as we exchanged greetings, raised sepulchral echoes. It was our first encounter with human kind since we had parted from the lock keeper at the head of the Lapworth locks the previous day.

We had now come within the outer suburban fringe of Birmingham, and between gaps in the neglected hedgerows we caught glimpses of new housing estates. The going had become steadily worse and even without such visual evidence we should have known we were back again in 'civilization' by the reefs of junk, old bicycle wheels and tyres, old perambulators, milk bottle crates and brick-bats, that lay in wait for us beneath every bridge. We had to drift through these bridges, otherwise our propeller would have become entangled in debris. Despite this precaution I had to spend some time hanging over *Cressy's* stern, knife in hand, hacking off the remains of an old car hood which had wrapped itself round our propeller blades.

Between the west end of the tunnel and the wooden Lifford drawbridge at King's Norton, which provided access to a new industrial estate, we were dragging and bumping over a litter-strewn bottom all the way and stirring up clouds of putrescent mud. It was the lunch hour and a little group of overalled men from a nearby factory were lounging on the drawbridge. Their presence was providential as we soon discovered. On sighting us, they obligingly pulled the bridge open and signalled us to come on. In doing so they must either have been optimistic or singularly unobservant, for the narrow channel beneath the bridge was thickly blocked with junk, as we soon found out when *Cressy* ground to a sudden stop. However, while two men continued to hold the bridge open, their fellows hauled manfully on bow and stern lines and managed to drag us over the obstruction. Beyond this, the canal was densely overgrown with weeds, but as we now had only three hundred yards to go to reach the stop lock, with its guillotine gates, which guarded the junction with the Worcester & Birmingham Canal, we ploughed on under our own power. By now our volunteer helpers, entering into the spirit of the thing, were accompanying us along the towpath with encouraging noises. It was as well that they did so for we needed their willing hands again when we stuck fast in the mouth of the stop lock.

Once inside the lock, I removed from our blades the Stratford Canal's final gift of two bicycle tyres and a length of old rope. Of the many miscellaneous objects that can become entangled in a propeller, tyres are the worst, as anyone who has ever tried cutting a tyre wire will readily appreciate. However, the job was done at last and the western guillotine gate opened like a camera shutter to reveal, framed in its aperture, a picture of the still, clear waters of the Worcester & Birmingham Canal. The sight was even more welcome than that of the Thames at Reading had been. To forge through disused canals may give one an exhilarating sense of pioneering achievement, but the constant risk of damaging the boat makes it an anxious business. Fortunately, with their two-inch oak planking and three-inch elm bottoms, wooden narrow boats are sturdy craft; but there are limits to the punishment they can take, particularly when they grow as old as *Cressy* was. A nightmare that haunted me during all the years I lived afloat was that I should one day knock a bottom up, causing the boat to sink with all our precious possessions on board. It was consequently a great relief to be heading *Cressy* south towards Tardebigge, knowing there was plenty of water under her bottom once more.

The uniformity later imposed by nationalization may be rational, but variety, however irrational it may appear, is nevertheless still the spice of life. The fact that our waterway system, like our railway system in pre-grouping days, was still owned by a multiplicity of old-established companies, each with its own by-laws, customs and traditions hallowed by time, added greatly to the charm and fascination of waterway travel. Canal boaters, too, were never the wandering 'water gypsies' of popular imagination but tended to stick to particular routes. Thus the boating families we had come to know best, the Hones, Humphreys, Harwoods, Wilsons, Skinners, Beauchamps, Townsends and Beecheys, had spent most of their lives on the Oxford Canal, boating coal from the Coventry area to Banbury or Oxford. Because the northern part of their respective 'runs' overlapped, these families were closely associated with – and in many cases related to – the much larger boating community that traded from the Midlands down the Grand Union Canal to London. So far as these boaters were concerned the Grand Union, Coventry and Oxford canals formed one parish in which everybody knew everybody else and where local news passed with astonishing speed from Sutton Stop to Sampson Road and from Bull's Bridge to Braunston. But now we had crossed the central watershed, and the canal we were entering was as unknown to this close-knit community as it was to us. I did not need the lettering 'W. & B. C.' on the cabin sides of moored maintenance boats or the heading 'Sharpness New Docks & Gloucester & Birmingham Navigation Company' on canal-side signs to remind me that I was now in the foreign waters of the Severn basin.

So, when the dark portal of the 2,750-yard West Hill tunnel loomed up ahead and I could discern no KEEP RIGHT sign such as I had become familiar with on the Grand Union system, I thought it would be prudent to discover what the native customs were in these parts before we ventured in. There was what I rightly took to be a canal lengthman's cottage perched on the hill directly over the tunnel's mouth, so we tied up while I climbed up to inquire. It was just as well that I did so. 'Keep left,' I was told. A possible subterranean collision accompanied by a great deal of profanity on both sides was thereby happily avoided.

While we passed through the long tunnel, Angela cooked our dinner by lamplight in the galley and the most appetizing smells wafted back to me through the open cabin doors. We emerged from the darkness into the golden light of a perfect late summer evening to find that we had left behind all traces of Birmingham's outer fringe. We ran past Hopwood and finally moored up beside Lower Bittall Reservoir. As we subsequently discovered, this large reservoir stretching away to the slopes of the Lickey Hills had to be built by the canal company as a condition of their Act in order to provide compensation water for the mill-owners on the little river Arrow whose headwaters the canal engineers proposed to tap. Not knowing this, we were mystified to find that the level of the reservoir was much lower than that of the canal. In fact, the canal embankment formed the reservoir dam so that from our mooring we could look out over a great glassy-smooth sheet of water. Through the thin mist that was already beginning to rise we could see that its mirror-like surface was speckled with hundreds of waterfowl: coot, moorhen, grebe and wild duck. Sometimes with sudden commotion a group of wild duck would take off to wheel against the sunset light, a small arrow-head, barbed with fast-beating wings. The evening air was still so warm that we dined in the open on *Cressy*'s foredeck. We stayed outside until the mist over the water had risen like a phantom tide to lap over the bank into the canal.

The following morning we were awakened by the familiar throbbing of a semi-diesel engine. We peered out eagerly, curious to see what strange 'foreign' craft this might be and who her owners. The mist over the canal was so thick that we could see nothing, but as the boat drew closer we could plainly hear above the noise of the engine two female voices conversing in the accents of Roedean or Westonbirt. Strange craft indeed! It could not be a working boat after all, we decided. Yet presently there glided into view the bluff bows of a narrow boat, low-laden in the water, and over the top of her side-cloths we could see a cargo of what looked like sacks of grain. What was stranger still, in her beautiful paintwork we recognized the unmistakable craftsmanship of our old friend Frank Nurser of Braunston Dock. We noticed her unfamiliar name, *Heather Bell*, before her unlikely crew had bid us good day and vanished once more into the mist.

Later, we came to know these two girls. The 'captain' was Daphne March whose brother had had *Heather Bell* built at Braunston just before the war with the intention of trading between his home town of Worcester and Birmingham. When, as a member of the R.N.V.R., he had gone on war service, Daphne had resolved to work the boat herself. Her companion was Kit Gayford, soon to achieve no small celebrity on the canals when she became responsible for training and supervising that intrepid band – so wrongly and rudely called the Idle Women – who volunteered to crew certain of the Grand Union Canal Carrying Co.'s fleet as their war service.

The sun soon dissolved the mist to shine down so brilliantly that we were able to eat our breakfast on deck. It was 4 September and our journey was almost over, for we knew that we had less than five miles of this beautiful summit level to cover in order to reach our destination. We sailed on into the dark tree-shaded mouth of Shortwood tunnel and were soon passing Tardebigge Old Wharf where we again plunged into the darkness of Tardebigge tunnel, cavern-like with its unlined walls of red sandstone. Emerging once more into the sunlight and rounding a bend, we saw before us for the first time our new home that was destined to become so familiar and so well-loved. It was exactly at noon that we put down our mooring lines at Tardebigge New Wharf. Apart from a couple of brief trips up to Bittall Reservoir and back with friends, *Cressy* would not move again for nearly five years.

Chapter 3

Eighteen Hundred Days in Tardebigge

In 1931, Miss Margaret Dickins, the daughter of a former vicar of Tardebigge who had held the living from 1855 to 1917, published *A Thousand Years in Tardebigge*, a book which, in its 180 pages, tells the story of the parish – it can scarcely be called a village – from the Saxon Taerdebicgan to the end of the Great War. Such a span of centuries made our brief sojourn in the parish shrink to an hour, meriting at most a single brief paragraph according to Miss Dickins's time-scale. Yet in spite of wartime difficulties and anxieties – and, indeed, to some extent because of them – these Tardebigge years turned out to be one of the most happy, full and fruitful periods of my life. It was for me a time of rapid spiritual and intellectual development. I nearly wrote 'maturity' instead of 'development' but realized that this would be an inappropriate word to describe someone who, intoxicated by his new powers and insights, felt confident that he held the key to all the world's ills, a key that could be used to build the new Jerusalem as soon as the war was over.

I marvel now that I could have accomplished so much and travelled so far (in a spiritual sense) in so short a time. Hence to write a coherent account of these years in one chapter entails as difficult a feat of compression as Miss Dickins achieved in her book. Let me first set the scene by describing the topography of Tardebigge and a little of what went on there. These things are important because I could never have lived there so contentedly had I not found the prospect so congenial. It was salutary to think that a landscape so near to Birmingham could remain so substantially unchanged, yet so it was.

44

The summit level of the Worcester & Birmingham Canal is 453 feet above sea level and extends for fourteen miles from Worcester Bar, Birmingham, to Tardebigge top lock. Because a considerable part of the Birmingham Canal Navigations (which the Worcester Canal joins) was constructed at the same height, this magical figure of 453 feet is usually referred to as the Birmingham Level. In the interests of water conservation and supply, the engineers of the new canal to Worcester (it was a comparative late-comer to the canal scene) were concerned to extend it southwards upon this level to the furthest feasible point. Tardebigge is that point. The southbound canal traveller gets no impression of the height of the Birmingham Level until he emerges dramatically from the darkness of Tardebigge Tunnel to find himself floating along the flank of a hill, a green promontory that juts southward into the blue sea of the vale. Three hundred yards from the mouth of the tunnel, the traveller comes to Tardebigge top lock, the first of that great flight of thirty locks by which the canal begins its descent to the Severn. It was a spot fifty yards from the head of this top lock that we selected for our mooring, so a landscape which the traveller only glimpses very briefly in passing, we were able to make a part of our lives, to be enjoyed in all weathers and all seasons.

To the right, a continuation of the low ridge called The Shaws that is pierced by the tunnel closed in the view to the north. Its cultivated slopes of red soil were patterned with a green corduroy of young fruit plantations, which whitened with blossom in springtime. Although this 'blowth' came markedly later here than in the vale below, these plantations escaped the pockets of deadly late frosts that in April, or even in May, are apt to fill the hollows of the vale with still pools of icy air, bringing despair to the fruit grower. To the west, the land fell steeply away from the very brink of the canal, the first focal point that the eye found to rest upon being the tall, crocketed red sandstone spire of Bromsgrove church about three miles away. The ugly, sprawling, brickish skirt about this old town was invisible thanks to the lie of the land and the many trees. That spire was the pivot of hills that often appeared so close to it yet were in fact far distant, being part of that border country west of Severn: the dark slopes of the Forest of Wyre by Bewdley; the Shropshire Clees; Woodbury Camp and the Abberley Hills above the valley of the Teme. And sometimes, on evenings when the air became crystal clear after rain, the remote shape of Black Mixen in Radnor Forest would appear on the far horizon.

All this country that Housman and Brett Young knew and loved lay spread before *Cressy's* windows. My fondness for hill country in general and for the Welsh Border in particular had not seemed to mix well with my love of canals. But I had too easily assumed that they were mutually exclusive, for here at Tardebigge the two were almost uniquely reconciled. When we picked Tardebigge from the map, we had certainly chosen better than we knew.

On the summit of the green ridge against the side of which we lay was the village church, built by Francis Hiorne of Warwick in 1777 out of the ruins of its predecessor following the collapse of the tower. Hiorne, who usually worked in the Gothic style, built here a classical tower topped by a spire of great elegance and extreme slenderness which soon became a familiar landmark. Seen from a distance it was difficult to believe that so delicate an object could be fashioned out of stone. We literally lay within its shadow, for on sunny winter mornings the steeple's shadow would fall across our deck, its point swinging like the style of a sundial over the meadows below.

The smooth green slope of the hill, and the particular relationship of the slender spire to the shapes and contrasting foliage of the surrounding trees made a composition so satisfying for the eye to rest upon and so perfectly complementary to the blue of the distant prospect below that it might have been contrived by Lancelot Brown or Humphrey Repton to gratify some noble patron. Yet although the manor of Tardebigge was owned by the Windsor family (later created Earls of Plymouth) from the Dissolution until shortly before we left the district, there is no evidence to suggest that this was so. Fortuitously, architect and civil engineer had collaborated with nature to provide for *Cressy* a landscape setting which suited my taste to perfection. And just as the eighteenth-century landscape architects would pander to the whims of their noble patrons by throwing in a hermit's cell complete with hermit, so to crown all, I had for good measure the company of a little community of craftsmen which reminded me of those I had known at Pitchill and Aldbourne.

Between *Cressy*'s stern and the mouth of the tunnel, on the New Wharf proper, was the principal maintenance depot for the Worcester & Birmingham Canal. It consisted of a huddle of workshops grouped around a dry dock, and a number of cottages built of local brick at widely different dates in the nineteenth century, yet all rubbing shoulders happily together. Here lived Mr Spiers, the Engineer of the canal, a shy, soft-spoken, gentle man with strange, frightened, restless eyes. In his youth, he had been a draughtsman with Belliss & Morcom, the famous firm of steam engine builders in Birmingham. A lonely man – he had lost his wife – Mr Spiers used often to visit us on the boat when we would talk engineering history by the hour. I remember once how he proudly showed me a beautiful coloured general arrangement drawing he had made of a Belliss vertical compound engine. Nominally, Mr Spiers was responsible for the management of workshops but in practice he seldom or never interfered with the four craftsmen, each a master in his own sphere, who between them ran the establishment. There was Mr Insull, the elderly blacksmith, portly and dignified; Percy Hawkins, the fitter and machinist who kept the nineteenth-century tools in the little machine shop so beautifully clean and oiled. It was only rarely that he had occasion to use them, but when he did so he often performed almost miraculous feats of improvisation and accuracy, such as boring a tapered hole in the boss of a new bronze propeller casting. Where I would have hesitated to undertake such a job on so ancient a lathe, Percy Hawkins set to work with complete assurance.

Then there was that short, thickset, jovial man, Tommy Hodges the boatbuilder, with his round red face glowing with exposure to winter weather in the open dock. He used to tell me that he could remember when twenty boatbuilders worked on the banks of this canal alone, yet now he was the sole survivor. But Tommy died before we left Tardebigge and we heard no more the regular thudding of his caulking mallet.

His last job was to replank an ice-breaker boat. As it lay in the dock, its curved oak ribs stripped of their rotten skin, it might have been the skeleton of some Viking ship. But it was George Bate, the fourth member of this quartet, whose skill I most admired. He was the lock-gate maker, and the wide doorway of his workshop opened on to a narrow quay so that a new-made lock-gate could be run out on a travelling pulley block and loaded directly into a maintenance boat. It did the heart good to watch George fashioning and assembling the massive oak principals of a frame gate: squaring the timbers, cutting tenon and mortise, drawing them together with powerful cramps and then finally bracing the whole with iron strap-work that had been made for him by Mr Insull. George was very proud of the fact that he was the latest representative of an unbroken succession of Bates who had worked on the Worcester & Birmingham ever since it was built. His shop was light and airy and always fragrant with the bitter tang of fresh hewn oak. It was also a very quiet and soothing place in which to linger, for George used no machines, even of a portable kind, after his timber had been squared in the saw-mill next door. Round its freshly whitewashed walls hung the tools of his trade, adze and shell-augur, not embalmed in some museum but, like that long pit-saw at Hungerford, still with the bloom of use upon them.

Bank Holiday week-ends, Easter, Whitsun and August, were the busiest times of the year for George Bate, for at such times a 'stoppage' on the canal would be announced so that new gates could be installed and any other necessary repair work to the locks carried out. At such times we would be awakened before dawn by the rumble of Worcestershire voices or the rattle of paddles at the top lock as there slid slowly past our cabin windows a maintenance boat laden with a new pair of gates and with all the paraphernalia necessary for installing them: sheer legs, pulley blocks, chains, coils of rope, a portable pumping set and lengths of hose for emptying a lock chamber somewhere on 'the thirty and twelve'.*

---

* So-called by George Bate and others because the famous Tardebigge flight of thirty locks was closely followed by twelve more between Stoke Prior and Dodderhill.

The only thing wrong with Tardebigge New Wharf was that it was teetotally dry. This had not always been so. The four-square Georgian brick building that was now the Plymouth Guesthouse, and whose windows overlooked the wharf, had once been known as the 'Plymouth Arms' until a bygone Earl of Plymouth, holding decided views on the evils of strong drink, caused its licence to be withdrawn. How many a boatman, having toiled to the summit of so prodigious a ladder of locks, must have cursed his lordship's scruples! But at least the boatmen were still able to slake their thirst at the 'Halfway House', so-called because it was situated beside the canal exactly half-way up the flight of thirty. This was our nearest pub and a pleasant walk it was down the towpath on a fine summer evening. The way led past Tardebigge Reservoir where, if you were lucky, you could watch great crested grebe performing their elaborate courtship ritual although they never appeared to breed. The reservoir was never used now and with its reedy, tree-bordered margins it more nearly resembled one of the Shropshire meres. It had been built by the canal company to store surplus storm water from the long summit level which was fed into the reservoir from just above the summit lock through a long culvert controlled by a paddle. In seasons of summer drought, water used to be pumped back to the summit from the reservoir by a beam pumping engine. Its engine house still stood near the reservoir though the engine had long ago been scrapped.

The 'Halfway' was a farm with a licence rather than an inn. This was just as well because on weekday evenings the takings must have been minimal; traffic on the canal had dwindled to a mere trickle and it was a true canal pub. It was clear that its original business had been with the towpath for it could only be reached with difficulty by the most narrow and tortuous of by-roads. Nevertheless, on Saturday evenings we could count upon finding a small but congenial company sitting round the scrubbed table in what had obviously once been the farm kitchen but was now the bar parlour. This company was made up of local farm labourers, smallholders and lengthmen or lock keepers from the canal with the addition of an occasional boatman or week-end fisherman. Most country pubs seem to favour some particular pastime or other; it may be darts, dominoes, table skittles, shove ha'penny or quoits, depending on what part of England you are in. On Saturday nights at the 'Halfway House', the favourite pastime was singing and a very jolly noise we made, sitting round by the light of a hanging paraffin lamp.

Master of ceremonies and star turn on these occasions was Jack Warner, a lock keeper whose cottage stood near the reservoir. A heavily built man of about seventy, his short legs were bowed and he walked with a rolling gait as though they were buckling beneath the weight of his body. With the heavy, sagging features of an ageing clown, Jack Warner was a 'natural'. He would get to his feet and treat the company to a rendering of some old music-hall song that included all the appropriate changes of expression, the graphic miming, the occasional dance steps and the inimitable way he could incite audience participation in the choruses. Though his repertoire was small, his audience never tired of it and the evening had seldom progressed very far before someone would call: 'Come on Jack, lad, gie us The Whitewash Brush,' and soon we would be roaring out the choruses which ended with the refrain:

> I put more whitewash on the old woman
> Than I put upon the parlour wall.

Jack Warner had a brother Joe who, though slightly the younger of the two, was much more staid and sober, perhaps because he was a married man whereas his brother was a widower. Joe Warner was our nearest neighbour as he and his wife lived in the cottage beside the top lock within fifty yards of our mooring. Though nominally the lock keeper, he also did labouring work at the New Wharf and each morning and evening he would clump past our boat in his heavy boots along the footpath that linked the lock with the wharf. Like his brother, Joe had a broad and musical Worcestershire dialect and his speech was peppered with unusual words and phrases. Thus he would always refer to wood pigeons as 'quice', an onomatopoeic word that I had never encountered before.

Thunder was always 'tempest': 'My word, tis 'ot,' he would exclaim, 'Reckon we shall ha' tempest afore night.'

The only new boatman friend we made while we were at Tardebigge was Charles Ballinger of Gloucester. To use the phraseology of the Oxford canal folk, he was the last of the 'west country boatmen', for as a young man helping his father he used to work through the Thames & Severn Canal and on to the upper Thames at Lechlade. On warm summer evenings when his low-laden boat was tied at the New Wharf, this long lean man with the worn and deeply tanned face used to hypnotize me with his stories of those far-off days until dusk deepened into darkness. He would shake his head over the chronic shortage of water on the summit of the Thames & Severn. So bad was it that, in the Canal's last days, the company provided what he called 'lightening boats' at each end of the great summit tunnel at Sapperton. He and his father used to offload part of their cargo into a lightening boat before setting out laboriously to 'leg' their way through the two-miles-long tunnel, towing the smaller boat behind them which, of course, had to be unloaded again into their own boat at the tunnel's end. But, as he pointed out, anything was better than being stuck on the bottom in those dark depths.

Charles Ballinger now owned four horse-boats, one of which he worked himself, all of them plying between his home port of Gloucester and the Midlands where they loaded coal. One of these was known as the 'match boat' because she carried 'England's Glory' matches from Gloucester to Birmingham on a regular contract. These boats were towed by tug between Gloucester Docks and Diglis, Worcester. At Diglis Basin, their captains picked up Company horses which hauled their boats to Tardebigge where the tunnel tug *Worcester* took over. This was a neat little craft with an outsize in Bollinder engines for which Percy Hawkins and his mate were responsible. When we first arrived at Tardebigge, there was a very beautiful steam tug, *Droitwich*, built by Abdela & Mitchell of Brimscombe, which was responsible for towage through West Hill tunnel, but eventually she needed re-tubing and this was never done as there was insufficient traffic to warrant two tugs. The single Tardebigge tug therefore had the task of towing through all three tunnels, after which the horses took over once more. This elaborate and costly arrangement of tugs and Company horses may have been all very well when dozens of horse-boats worked over the route, but now that their number had shrunk to four only it had obviously become hopelessly uneconomic. I used to reflect ruefully that it would have paid the Company handsomely to give Charles Ballinger an expensive 'golden handshake', although I was delighted that they never did so. All the rest of the traffic, such as it was, was self-propelled and, apart from the *Heather Bell*, which we have already encountered, it consisted entirely of single motor boats of the Severn & Canal Carrying Company's fleet: steel boats with drab paintwork of blue and white, some of the ugliest and clumsiest narrow boats ever built. They were crewed usually with pathetic incompetence by tatterdemalion families which the Company had obviously recruited from 'off the bank', as the boatmen say. It was sadly clear that this once flourishing carrying company was now nearing the end of its life.

So much for the small world to which I returned at evening. Of my work I need say little except that it provided me with instructive first-hand experience of the engineering industry of the Midlands, ranging from such large plants as Wolseley Motors at Ward End, Birmingham, or Guy Motors at Wolverhampton, to the smallest of back street press shops in Deritend or Aston. One interesting fact that I discovered at this time was how profoundly even the largest of works could be affected by the personality of the man in control. One could very quickly sense whether the atmosphere in a particular shop was happy or unhappy, while a few moments' conversation with the managing director almost invariably supplied the explanation.

I had no intention of wearing out my father's Alvis in the Government service so, soon after we arrived at Tardebigge, I bought a 1938 Austin 'Big Seven' saloon and returned the Alvis to its home garage for the duration. This meant that both Alvises were now in hibernation at Stanley Pontlarge awaiting better times. The Austin was such a terrible little car in every way that at first I felt ashamed to be seen driving it. It used to suffer from bouts of acute clutch slip due to the oil that found its way through the back main bearing. Carbon tetrachloride was the best palliative for this. I would head for the nearest branch of Woolworths, buy a bottle of Thawpit and pour it into the clutch housing. This effected a temporary cure and by such expedients I kept the car running until the end of the war when I could not wait to be rid of it. It is ironical to reflect that at this time the Austin was the most expensive single object I had ever purchased, *Cressy* herself not excepted.

By the Ministry I was known as an 'Isolated Technical Assistant'. My desk on *Cressy* was my 'office' although I also had the use, whenever I needed it, of a bare, ink-stained trestle table, a chair and a telephone in an office on the sixth floor of the C.M.L. building in Great Charles Street, Birmingham. Although I naturally became very familiar with the city during these years, it never endeared itself to me in any way. I used to feel oppressed by the thorough-going Philistinism of the place. It was so painfully evident that it was the creation of people who, for a hundred years or more, had pursued the making of money with completely single-minded devotion. Yet I admit this experience did later awaken in me a certain nostalgia for the older Birmingham, with its jewellery and gun quarters and its clanging trams reeling like galleons down narrow, setted streets or rounding impossibly sharp curves with a sudden shriek of protesting wheel flanges.

The most onerous and unproductive part of my desk work was the completion of a weekly claim form for travelling expenses and subsistence. This form had been devised by a mind exclusively concerned to circumvent the possibility of any falsification, accidental or deliberate, on the part of the applicant. The result was such a masterpiece of complexity that to fill it in honestly was impossible, short of adding pages of explanatory notes. Hence the form was always referred to by the irreverent 'temporaries' in my Department as the Swindle Sheet. It revealed the same careful, conscientious and humourless bureaucratic mentality that had not only caused every single sheet of the paper rolls in the lavatories at C.M.L. building to be rubber-stamped 'Government Property' but had placed a typed notice over each fitment which read: PLEASE EXERCISE THE UTMOST ECONOMY IN THE USE

OF PAPER. To this, almost inevitably, some scatological wag had added: 'Please use both sides.'

The furthest afield that my work took me now was a fortnightly visit to the Sentinel Waggon Works at Shrewsbury, with an occasional call in the Wellington neighbourhood on the way. As it was usually late by the time I left Sentinels and as I was due in Wolverhampton the following morning, it was obviously better on such occasions to spend a night in Shropshire instead of consuming precious petrol in returning to the boat. For this purpose I picked the 'Valley Hotel' at Coalbrookdale and was thus introduced to the Severn Gorge and the ancient industrial district of Shropshire. The first time I came to the 'Valley Hotel', having picked it with the aid of an ordnance map and an A.A. guide, it was late autumn and darkness had already fallen; yet I knew at once that I had hit upon a very special place, for as soon as I walked into the bar of the hotel my eye was caught and held by three large and handsome coloured engravings of local scenes which hung on the walls. As I subsequently discovered, these were three of a set of six, engraved from originals by George Robertson and published by the brothers Boydell in 1788. One was a romantic landscape featuring the slender arc of the famous first iron bridge against a towering background of hanging woods, while the subject of the second was John Wilkinson's Broseley Ironworks. Here the same romantic landscape of the Severn Gorge had been rudely invaded and blighted by the dragon of industrial revolution, breathing fire and foul smoke from furnace and stack. But it was the third picture that I thought the most striking. It was titled 'The Inside of a Smelting-house at Broseley'. It depicted a building which might have been a tithe barn were it not for the tall wooden pivoting crane in the centre of the picture, a triangle of timbers as massive as lock-gate balance beams. The main source of light in this building came from a rectangular opening to the right of the crane which resembled the mouth of hell, so fierce was the glare that issued from it. This was the fore-part of a blast furnace from which molten iron was being tapped. Three figures, one sharply lit, the other two seen in silhouette, directed the white-hot stream through the sand of

the floor and into the runners of a pig-bed in the right foreground. In telling contrast to this fiery bedlam, an open
archway to the extreme left of the picture revealed a tantalizing
glimpse of a night landscape of calm serenity in which a full
moon had just risen above a bank of white cloud.

It seemed to me a prophetic warning of the greater desola-
tion to come that such crude but dramatic manifestations of
the second Iron Age should appear in one of the most romantic-
ally beautiful landscapes in Britain. It is a pity that the originals
of these engravings have disappeared, because George Robertson was one of the first artists to grasp the significance of this
violent contrast and to give expression to it in paint. He was
by no means the last. Many artists who appreciated the then
unsullied beauty of the English landscape, but had hitherto
taken it for granted as part of man's natural birthright, were
drawn to the Severn Gorge and Coalbrookdale by a fearful
fascination. They sought to express in paint and in words the
strangely ambivalent feelings aroused by the dramatic contrast
between the fuming, flaming clangour of the ironworks and
their idyllic setting of wooded hills and streams.

In the course of subsequent visits when, in the long summer
evenings, I explored 'the Dale' and the Ironbridge Gorge
on foot, I came fully to share the feelings of those bygone
artists. Although the famous iron bridge still spans the Severn
and men still cast iron in the foundry at Coalbrookdale, the
blast furnaces are dead; Wilkinson's Bedlam Furnace is no
more than a cold ruin of crumbling, blackened brick beneath a
kindly veil of creeper. Yet the whole area seemed to me to be
haunted. Everywhere I was reminded of the fierce activity of
former days, and every stick and stone of the place seemed to
have absorbed something of its white hot violence. It was here
that Abraham Darby the First succeeded in smelting iron
with coke instead of charcoal; here that the first iron hull was
made and launched, the first iron steam engine cylinders and
the first iron rails were cast; here that the first steam locomotive was built to the design of Richard Trevithick. Yet I
needed no such recital of historical facts to tell me that it was
here that it had all begun. I could feel it on my pulses; and, if I
needed any reminder, the great black semi-circle of Darby's

iron bridge, springing over Severn, spoke to me more eloquently than any history book.

At that time there were still some astonishing survivals to be seen in this part of Shropshire. I once had occasion to visit the Horsehay Ironworks which stands high up under the Wrekin. In the open works yard I saw men busy making steel invasion barges in preparation for 'D' Day. This sight was remarkable enough in such an improbable situation, but to make it the more extraordinary these barge builders were kept supplied with materials by a horse-drawn plate tramway – waggons with flangeless wheels running on cast-iron flanged rails, or 'ginny rails' as they still call them in Shropshire. Nor was this all. When I left Horsehay, I took the road towards Coal-brookdale. Imagine my astonishment when I beheld, just to the left of the road, a scene which, though very familiar to me from early engravings, I never expected to see in actuality. It was a working 'ginny pit'. A horse, plodding round in a circle, was turning the wooden barrel of the gin to wind a corve of coal up the shaft of the pit. Some sceptical readers may think that on that particular day I was suffering from hallucinations but, improbable though it may seem, my recollection of this astonishing sight is perfectly clear.

Early one summer evening I was standing beneath the arch of the iron bridge admiring its construction when I was accosted by a most remarkable man. He was wearing buttoned cloth gaiters, a pair of cord breeches, a green cloth waistcoat trimmed with braid, a bright red neckerchief and a cap clapped flatly on the back of his head. His grey eyes were keen and deep-set, his face as weathered by exposure as a gypsy's and he had the proud profile of a Roman emperor. His name was Harry Rogers. No sooner had we introduced ourselves, it seemed, than we were on easy Christian name terms. Harry made coracles in a little wooden shed with a slip-way running down from it to the Severn within the shadow of the iron bridge. Officially, he was a rabbit catcher, but I suspect this was a cover. It did not explain those mysterious nocturnal expeditions when at nightfall he would slip away soundlessly downstream in his coracle, not to return until the small hours of the morning.

Harry's shed by the river was filled and festooned with a purposeful clutter of objects: coils of rope, bundles of netting, rabbit snares and other miscellanea less easily identifiable. There were also stocks of the materials from which he made his coracles: lengths of sawn ash lath, rolls of coarse canvas, pots of tar and pitch. Maybe a new coracle frame, looking rather like a huge scuttle or skep basket such as were then still made in the Forest of Wyre, was building upon the floor. Here, leaning against the workbench or sitting in the doorway in the westering sunlight, we used to talk away many a summer's evening. He spoke in an extremely broad and somewhat harsh-sounding dialect which surprised me at first; it was so utterly unlike the soft speech of western Shropshire with which I was familiar. It seemed to me more closely akin to Black Country dialect and led me to speculate whether, when that area succeeded Shropshire as the centre of the new iron age, the men of Coalbrookdale and district had migrated thither. We talked of many things. He told me that the secret of the iron hardness of old oak timbers was that the trees were never allowed to lie in the bark when felled but were stripped of that bark for the tanneries while they were still green. He told me why his cottage behind the shed was called 'The Victory'. The local Council had placed a demolition order on it and had crassly offered him a new council house at Madeley on the top of the Hill. 'I to'd 'em,' he said, 'that afore I'd leave Siven they'd 'ave t' carry me feet form'st.' So battle had been joined. Finally he and his son had set to work to rebuild their cottage completely, and its new name celebrated the defeat of local bureaucracy. He also told me the sad story of the last trading barge to be seen on the Severn north of Bewdley. She had loaded a cargo of earthenware pipes at Jackfield, but had come to grief at Bridgnorth where her cargo had to be taken off. She was then bought by a man in Shrewsbury for conversion into a stationary houseboat. Harry's father, with the assistance of his young son and a couple of horses, had then undertaken delivery to her new owner. Upstream to Shrewsbury, the river had long been disused for navigation, and Harry recalled with a wicked chuckle that the local landowners were not amused when they broke down their hedges to make a way for the horses, claiming the ancient right to navigate 'the King's high stream of Severn' without let or hindrance.

I liked best Harry's story of the would-be suicide. He was returning late at night in his coracle from some nefarious expedition when he saw, dimly outlined against the stars, a figure standing behind the high railings on top of the iron bridge. In a loud voice he was proclaiming his intention to do away with himself. Harry landed noiselessly at his slip, crept up behind the unsuspecting suicide and suddenly in a stern voice called out 'Hey, stop tha' 'ollerin', I'll gie thee a leg oop.' "Ee didn't arf run,' commented Harry. 'Reckon 'ee thought it was owd Nick 'isself as'd come fer 'im.'

While we talked, his keen eyes strayed constantly towards the river, ever on the look-out for a likely piece of flotsam. After a flood his slipway would be littered with the objects he had salvaged: a substantial tree trunk; a couple of stout fencing posts; part of a landing stage; an old punt. He used to boast that Severn supplied him with all his winter fuel. In a time of high flood, when the gorge brimmed with an angry torrent of swirling brown waters, I have watched admiringly as he manoeuvred his frail coracle with supremely confident skill to capture with a line a large floating log and bring it in to his slip. He was a man who had adapted himself to Severn as naturally and as perfectly as any otter or salmon.

I finally persuaded Harry to build a coracle for me and when it was finished, I bore it proudly home to Tardebigge on the roof of the Austin. On summer evenings in the still waters of the canal, I mastered the difficult art of propelling it with a single paddle in the direction in which I wanted to go instead of spinning round like a teetotum, providing the locals with much innocent entertainment in the process. Like riding a bicycle it was all a question of balance. Once you lost that balance, the coracle instantly turned turtle and its occupant found himself struggling in the water, his head trapped beneath it in the large bubble of air it held as in some dark diving bell. I still have that coracle. It is a constant reminder of Ironbridge and of one of the most remarkable characters I have ever been lucky enough to know. I cherish his memory dearly. For me, Harry Rogers seemed to incarnate the very spirit of Severn, a spirit infinitely more ancient than the ironworks that once flamed upon its banks.

I sometimes used to feel guilty about my work for the Ministry of Supply. It was the first 'white collar' job I had ever had and it was also the best paid. I was conscientious and knew that I was achieving as good results as most of my colleagues, and probably better than some. Yet after my experience on the shop floor it did seem to me to be what my workmates would have called a cushy job. There was no doubt in my mind that the work I had been doing at the Aldbourne Foundry, because it had called for a far greater expenditure of creative effort and skill, was the more intrinsically valuable. That it was so meagrely rewarded seemed contrary to common sense. Nevertheless, these years with the Ministry were not wasted; they yielded their quota of valuable experiences. I should never have visited Coalbrookdale and met Harry Rogers for one thing, for with petrol supplies restricted to essential purposes, I was luckier than most people in the extent to which I was able to travel about the Midland shires.

For all private and domestic journeys, of course, we had to depend on a public transport system that today no longer exists. My annual leaves we usually spent at Llanthony Abbey in the Black Mountains, and these recurring visits affected me so deeply that they were easily the most potent single influence upon my life during this period.

The first of them was in September 1940, while we were still at Hungerford. We were able then to travel by car, crossing the Severn by the Beachley–Aust ferry, but subsequent journeys from Tardebigge had to be made by rail to Llanvihangel Crucorney station and thence on foot for seven miles up the Vale of Ewyas with our belongings on our backs. This country, and in particular this valley of the Honddu, had made a deep impression upon me as a small boy. Moreover, with the passing of the years my childish memories of it had not faded but sharpened, so much so that when war broke out and the world seemed to come crashing about our ears I felt an irresistible urge to revisit this country of my childhood. On our first visit I had felt uneasy. Would I be disillusioned and disappointed? Might I not find that a magic which had worked so powerfully upon my childish imagination could no longer be received by my blunted adult senses? I need not have worried; experience soon proved that this homing instinct had been right.

As we walked beneath the arching hazels in the deep lanes of the valley floor or along the high ridges of the mountain walls that enclosed it; as we climbed the Gospel Pass, retracing that same green track by which I had first come to the valley by horse-drawn waggonette from Cusop as a small boy, I realized that remembered beauties were no figment of childish fancy. They were real and had not changed. To know that what had spoken to me as a child could speak just as eloquently to me now was a moving and exalting experience. But whereas in my childhood I had taken for granted that what I apprehended was eternal, now it appeared the more poignant and precious because, as a man, I had learned that my species alone possessed the power to disfigure or to destroy it utterly. Man could, if he willed it so, drown the landscape of this valley, these flowering meadows, those tall trees and small stone farms, fathoms deep beneath the waters of a reservoir, silencing forever the voices of its streams; he could mar the majestic profile of the mountains with a dark and deadening blanket of alien conifers leaving the barren earth beneath to leach away; or he could trample them under the arrogant steel feet of marching pylons.

Once we walked over the mountain ridge into the adjoining valley of Gwynne Fawr and saw with sinking hearts that its slopes had been planted with regimented ranks of conifers. The lines of the unclimbable wire fences that bordered these new plantations, so wantonly blocking ancient tracks and footpaths, had obviously been arbitrarily ruled by a hand utterly unmoved by any tenderness or reverence for the lovely natural folds and curves of the landscape. Within the confines of this vegetable concentration camp stood noble trees of native hardwood wearing their green leaves for the last time; for their bark had been ringed and they had been brutally left to die. The sight filled me with impotent rage.

For the rest, the landscape of the Black Mountains was still the same as it had been in my childhood; but the fate of Gwynne Fawr, as an example of man's arrogance, his folly and his greed, now made its beauties seem as ephemeral as a rose, and so the more keenly to be apprehended and treasured.

One occasion, especially, has stayed in my mind. I was looking out of a window of our candle-lit bedroom high in one of the south towers of the Abbey. This window looked across the roofless ruin of the Abbey church to where the high altar had once stood. The summer night was perfectly still and calm, and a full moon had just risen above the dark protective wall of Hatterall hill. The clipped turf below was lightly silvered with dew, and upon it the nave columns and arches cast shadows almost as dark and substantial as they themselves appeared. In this pattern of substance and shadow, the aspirations and the craftsmanship of long forgotten men, the loveliness of the landscape and the celestial beauty of the night seemed to become inseparable parts of one whole so majestical that no words of mine can describe it. I can only attempt to convey the effect it had upon me. It was no longer possible to believe, as does the materialist, that what I saw revealed no creative purpose but was merely the chance by-product of blind chaos. I became convinced that this was not so. Nor did the argument that all beauty is in the eye of the beholder shake this conviction. For even if it were true that what I saw before me was merely a pattern imposed upon a formless void by my own mind and senses, then from what mysterious source, I wondered, did such a vision spring? Reality or vision, the revelation remained. I am no mystic, yet I think I had come near to understanding what Henry Vaughan meant when he wrote:

> I saw Eternity the other night
> Like a great ring of pure and endless light,
> All calm, as it was bright . . .

In our long and often painful pilgrimage from birth to death, most of us set out with the notion that eventually we shall find a key to the mystery of life; surely there must be a wise man somewhere who, if only we can find him, knows all the answers? We eye our fellow pilgrims hopefully, wondering

from what source they derive the strength to stride so purpose-
fully upon their way despite the tragedies and misfortunes
that are man's common lot. Failing to find this wise man in
the flesh, we then seek him at second-hand in the written
word. Often such a quest ends in the acceptance of a particular
credo which offers consoling, over-simplified solutions to every
problem, provided only that we suspend our own critical judgement and reject or ignore such of those lessons of experience
which conflict with that one true faith. I ran such a course,
but by this time in my life I had reached a point where I
realized that no one person and no one religion or philosophy
could claim a monopoly of truth; that truth was something to
be distilled from personal experience, to be felt along the
pulses but never to be purchased second-hand; the pursuit of
it a quest that must continue to my life's end. Deliberately to
choose such a hard road may sound proud and arrogant. In
fact I have never scorned or rejected the sayings or writings of
those older, wiser or more experienced than I am; and I have
known nothing more exciting and stimulating than to discover my own experience confirmed or enlarged in this way.
But for me, doctrine has always been accepted or rejected by the
touchstone of personal experience and not the other way round.

Now, as a fruit of experiences such as the one I have just
tried to describe, I conceived an idea of the natural world – or,
indeed, of the whole universe including man himself – as a vast
ordered system of interdependent parts. For someone like
myself, with an engineering cast of mind, I was tempted to
substitute the word 'mechanism' for 'system' although, as I
knew only too well, this was apt to be a misleading analogy.
For a so-called mechanistic view of the universe generally
implies materialism, whereas in my case this was very definitely
not so. For I found it impossible to conceive even the simplest
of mechanisms, let alone one so infinitely complex in operation
and so beautifully ordered, which had not been consciously
designed. It seemed to me that in this vast and elaborate
scheme of things, man occupied a position uniquely privileged,
and therefore responsible and hazardous. He alone was at
once inside and outside the system. On the one hand, as a
creature, he was a part of the mechanism and so ultimately

governed by its laws; on the other, as a man, he was uniquely equipped to comprehend it, to unravel and understand some, though not all, of the complex working principles by which it operated. It was knowledge so gained that gave man the power to tinker with the works, with consequences that could lead to total disaster.

Once conceived, this view of the universe seemed infinitely exciting; it influenced all my thought, gave to everything I read – and I now began to read much more – a new meaning. What was more important, it explained, to my own satisfaction at all events, the deep dichotomy in my own nature; why my consuming interest in things mechanical so often conflicted with my passionate feeling for the beauties of the natural world. This is why, as I wrote at the beginning of this chapter, I look back on the war years that I spent at Tardebigge as among the happiest and most fruitful of my life.

Through my friend Sam Clutton, we had acquired a small clavichord which was, I believe, the first instrument to be built by Alec Hodsdon of Lavenham who was later to become celebrated as a maker of harpsichords. It was the only type of keyboard instrument that would fit into the small compass of a canal boat cabin and I contrived a folding stand for it, so we could easily stow it away if need be. The clavichord's small and subtle voice which makes it unsuitable for public performance was perfectly suited to the confined space of our boat cabin. Of an evening, Angela would play some simple, plaintive little piece by William Byrd or John Bull while I would sit reading, or, preoccupied with my thoughts, gazing out of the deep windows of our cabin while the sun went down behind the Abberley Hills and shadows began to thicken in the vale below. After days spent in Birmingham or Wolverhampton, at such times *Cressy*'s cabin with its familiar bookshelves seemed mercifully isolated from the fretful fever of human affairs. Here, so it seemed to me, I could step aside from the world for a few hours and regard it objectively as though from some other planet. Illusory though this sense of detachment and isolation might be, it acted as a great spiritual and mental stimulus which I found immensely valuable.

My historical self-education had hitherto been confined to

the period of Britain's Industrial Revolution because this seemed to me to be the most significant and fateful movement in the history of man. Now, armed with new insights, I began to range much more widely in social history, and particularly in the histories of religion, philosophy and science, in an attempt to chart the currents of thought which had brought that Revolution about. In doing so I discovered to my surprise that my thinking was much more closely akin to medieval ideas about the cosmos and of man's place in it than to any subsequent scientific view of the universe. It seemed to me astonishing that men, so woefully ignorant of the laws by which 'the great machine' operated that they could believe that sun and planets revolved about a flat earth, should, none the less, have succeeded in arriving intuitively at an elaborate concept or model of universal order which rang prophetically true. Taken literally, the figures they employed to express and explain this concept of order, the chain of being, the correspondences, the music of the spheres and the cosmic dance, make so much scientific gibberish; yet, at the deeper level of poetic imagery and metaphor, such figures struck me as being profoundly meaningful. This conception of cosmic order was essentially moral because the medieval mind saw it as an ideal model for human society. It drew parallels between the natural order and man's social order, and judged the latter accordingly. It believed that, in so far as the lives of men, individually or collectively, were true to this analogy, goodness and harmony prevailed and, conversely, evil and chaos were the inevitable accompaniment of non-conformity.

It so happened that at this time (1943) the late Dr E. M. W. Tillyard's book *The Elizabethan World Picture* was first published. So far as I was concerned, its appearance could not have been more timely. In it Dr Tillyard shows how, despite the new currents of Renaissance thought which were beginning to flow in Elizabethan England, a 'world picture' of cosmic order inherited from the Middle Ages was still tacitly accepted and so continued to exercise a profound influence over the thought of the period. I owe a great deal to this book; not least, it enlarged my understanding of the plays of Shakespeare, making them seem immeasurably greater and more meaningful. Once one accepts the medieval concept of universal order, then the histories and the tragedies of Shakespeare become so many object-lessons on the consequences of violating that order, no matter whether it be through the sins of pride (Lear), ambition (Macbeth) or jealousy (Othello). *Macbeth* had long been my favourite play, but now it seemed to take on an entirely new dimension as I saw in Macbeth's undoing the image of modern man.

It is a measure of the greatness and universal quality of Shakespeare's art that, like life itself, it should be capable of bearing so many different interpretations. We look at his plays, as at life, through the polarized spectacles of our own 'world picture', seeing in them only what we expect to see. Thus current productions reflect the bleak existentialist view of man, and their weight of meaning is, in my view, immeasurably diminished thereby. Yet I take heart from the fact that although Dr Tillyard's book was not reprinted for twenty years, it has now been reprinted three times in paperback edition, a belated popularity which may reflect impending change.

Implicit in the notion of cosmic order was the belief that this world could become a paradise provided man recognized and obeyed the laws of that order and so steered clear of the seven deadly sins. Once I had grasped this, the story of Adam and Eve, which had previously seemed to me no more than a quaint and scientifically absurd fable, now suddenly assumed a new and tremendously significant weight of meaning: that paradise, where man had once walked naked and unashamed, was firmly rooted upon earth and was not in some remote and abstract hereafter in the skies. And ever since man's own follies had driven him out of this earthly paradise he had been haunted by ancient race memories, to remind him of the magnitude of that loss; by dreams, by intimations of beauty, or by that sense of sorrow, born of our inability to savour it sufficiently fully, to which the contemplation of natural beauty moves us. If, as has been said, such beauty does indeed reside solely in the eye of the beholder, then may not its apprehension be due to the mysterious working of some unbelievably ancient genetically inherited faculty, reminding us so poignantly of an Eden long lost?

Pursuing such lines of thought, it seemed to me that man's material progress had been accompanied by the gradual failure and loss of this ancient vision until, in the orthodox religious view, this world became merely a dreary battleground of sin, temptation and toil, its beauties and joys the seductions of the devil, in which man was abjured to 'fight the good fight' in the hope of earning his reward in a nebulous hereafter becoming, one must suppose, uncomfortably crowded. It was in the emergence of this bleak, puritanical view of the world as a kind of purgatory where each individual must strive for personal salvation against every kind of sensual temptation that I believed I had found the key to all that had followed, including the ultimate defeat of organized religion by scientific materialism. For to counsel the rejection of the world along with the flesh and the devil seemed to me a blasphemy which had completely changed man's 'world picture' and led inevitably to a fundamental change in the relationship between man and the natural world. Whereas before, the concept of human society modelled in a cosmic order implied a partnership between man and nature that was based on wonder and humility, man's attitude could now be summed up in the increasingly popular phrase 'the conquest of nature'. Humility was succeeded by *hubris*; the ancient vision of a lost paradise on earth faded and man declared total war upon his world. And because one of the first rules of war is to denigrate your enemy, the natural world was now seen to be merely the chance product of the interaction of blind forces. To win command over these forces and to harness them in the service of a campaign of wholesale rapine and rape thereafter became man's sole concern. There was no conflict here with the old puritanical religious concept of fighting the good fight through a vale of tears; only the desired goal had changed. The notion of individual reward in a mythical hereafter gave place to an unquestioning faith in material progress. In other words, ultimate victory in man's campaign against nature would spell Utopia on earth. As we are now very belatedly discovering, however, this vision of a man-made paradise is as illusory as that of the earlier hereafter which it superseded. Had we not been so beguiled by the scientific messiahs of material progress, forever promising jam tomorrow, we might have realized sooner that the only end product of total war is a scorched and pillaged earth, an uninhabitable desert.

I saw in the publication of Charles Darwin's *Origin of Species* the scientific shot which had finally scuppered the ship of organized religion. The notions of 'nature red in tooth and claw' and of 'the survival of the fittest' appeared fully to sanction man's conquest of nature, for by thus taking up arms against her, man was simply acting in accordance with these inexorable natural laws which had existed since time began. To prove himself the fittest to survive in a general free-for-all, with no holds barred, appeared to be man's natural role. To a religion which had lost its vision and clung doggedly to a literal interpretation of the scriptures, the Darwinian theory dealt a fatal blow from which it has never recovered.

I read of this century-old Darwinian controversy with absolute incredulity. Although science is dedicated to the pursuit of truth, scientific 'laws' invariably turn out either to be false or to be, at best, misleading half truths. The reason for this apparent paradox is that the pursuit of truth is an endless journey into undiscovered country. There is always more to be found round the next corner which is capable of altering our whole perspective of the road we have travelled. What had seemed to one generation of scientists an unalterable law is proved invalid by the next. So it is with Darwinism. The theory was correct, but the survival of the fittest is by no means the only law governing the evolutionary process, and we have since found that the genetic mechanisms governing evolution are infinitely more complex and subtle than Darwin supposed. But, even so, the formulation of a principle by which the mechanism of creative purpose operated should never have induced men to jump to the conclusion that because there was a mechanism there could not be any sentient agent of that purpose. This seemed to me a complete *non sequitur*. The only thing that Darwin's shot had sunk was the myth that the world had been created complete in seven days in a geologically recent past.

Of the religious writers that I discovered at this time it was the so-called Cambridge Platonists of the seventeenth century, especially Henry Vaughan and Thomas Traherne, who appealed to me most strongly, and it was with a shock of surprise that I found that both Vaughan and Traherne had known the Black Mountain country of my childhood and had obviously been influenced by it. Neither man subscribed to the gloomy, puritanical view of the world that became fashionable in their day. On the contrary they enjoyed its manifold beauties with wonder and humility as revelations of creative purpose. I felt that had they lived in the nineteenth century their vision and belief would not have been lost or shaken by any scientific discoveries of the methods by which that purpose operated. Traherne, in a passage which I quoted in the previous volume of this autobiography, specifically distinguishes between the world of men and the world of nature; 'leave the one that you may enjoy the other,' he exhorts. This is but a short step from the medieval doctrine that sought to bring the two worlds closer together by seeing the natural order as providing a set of rules for the guidance of man in shaping his social order.

It is easy to record outward happenings; it is far more difficult honestly to chart the spiritual progress that accompanies them, and which in part influences those events and is in part influenced by them. However, I have tried to summarize as faithfully as I can how far I travelled in the world of thought and imagination during the war years. It will, I think, help to explain future events and my reactions to them.

Chapter 4

Getting into Print

In my new-found philosophy I believed I had at last found the key to problems that had troubled me all my life. The effect that this discovery had upon me was intensely exhilarating, not to say intoxicating. Conundrums over which I had puzzled in vain were suddenly solved; what had appeared meaningless and chaotic fragments now became parts of an ordered pattern; the natural world had never seemed to me more beautiful. I cannot define and explain this euphoric state of mind better than by quoting a passage from Thomas Traherne's *Centuries of Meditations*:

> You never enjoy the world aright, till you so love the beauty of enjoying it, that you are covetous and earnest to persuade others to enjoy it. And so perfectly hate the abominable corruption of men in despising it, that you had rather suffer the flames of Hell than willingly be guilty of their error. There is so much blindness and ingratitude and damned folly in it. The world is a mirror of infinite beauty, yet no man sees it. It is a Temple of Majesty, yet no man regards it. It is a region of Light and Peace, did not men disquiet it. It is the Paradise of God. It is more to man since he is fallen than it was before. It is the place of Angels and the Gate of Heaven.

I, too, felt that I was enjoying the world aright and became covetous and earnest to persuade others to enjoy it with me. I was the more encouraged to do this by the interregnum of war and its effect upon society. When life is forced by desperate emergency out of its normal peacetime channels, when men and women are called upon to face common perils and hardships, their old rivalries and antagonisms tend to be forgotten and they become 'members one of another'. In such an atmosphere of goodwill it was easy to believe that 'the bad old days' of the nineteen-thirties would never return; that men had now surely seen the error of their ways and would start building a new and better world as soon as the war was over.

In this new mood of certitude and optimism I began furiously to write, oblivious of that rejected manuscript which lay forgotten in a suitcase beneath our bed. Considering that I could only write in my spare time, I marvel now that I accomplished so much in so short a space of time. Leafing through a scrap book of old and yellowing press cuttings, I am amazed that I ever had the temerity to write with such oracular assurance on so wide a variety of subjects. I aired my views in the 'little magazines', in *Horizon, Kingdom Come,* and *Voices,* and took part in many controversies in the correspondence columns of the weeklies. For *Horizon* I wrote an article which dealt with the tyranny of the machine over man and forecast that in the future a better educated generation would inevitably rebel against the stupifying monotony which it imposed; for *Kingdom Come,* 'Imagination and the Dramatic Art', a plea for an uncluttered stage and a more imaginative use of lighting in place of elaborate sets; for *Voices,* 'Letter to a Surrealist', a lengthy reply countering a series of articles expounding the surrealist philosophy. But the main object of my attack was the baneful effect of modern technology and economics on world ecology, particularly as applied to agriculture. In this battle I joined forces with Lord Portsmouth, Sir Albert Howard and H. J. Massingham.

My correspondence with H. J. Massingham began with a 'fan' letter from me and soon developed into a regular and frequent exchange of letters over a period of years in which we freely set down our views and ideas. I have never maintained such an intimate and lengthy correspondence either before or since and found it extraordinarily stimulating. Such a meeting of minds is a rare pleasure which has now been made almost impossible by the relentless pressures of modern life. Because they allow us no time to translate our thoughts on to paper, letter writing becomes merely a necessary and generally

unwelcome chore, the result a brief and colourless short-hand
of facts and banalities. One wonders how many of those bulky
volumes of posthumous correspondence our generation will
produce. Very few, I would guess.

In addition to all this ephemeral writing and correspondence
I found time to set down my ideas on paper in a book which
proclaimed that our machine civilization was heading for
disaster unless it changed its course. I concluded that: 'the
wastage of human and natural resources which an acquisitive
society necessarily incurs, leads logically towards barbarism
and the exhaustion of those resources'. While I explained how
I thought this fatal course might be corrected, I came to the
conclusion that such a correction could only be made by a
generation which had received a more enlightened education.
In other words, ambitious and precocious though it was, it
offered no quick Utopian panacea. I took the book's title *High
Horse Riderless*, from the closing lines of a poem by W. B.
Yeats in which he laments the passing of an older and more
stable society:

> But all is changed, that high horse riderless
> Though mounted in that saddle Homer rode
> Where the swan drifts upon a darkling flood.

A great, riderless horse; it made me think of the fabulous
horses, the broken columns and the desolate and strangely
menacing landscapes that I had seen in certain paintings by
Chirico which I had admired on the walls of a friend's house
near Hungerford. Though I could not fathom the precise
meaning of Yeats's use of the image, it seemed to me an
exactly appropriate one for a technological civilization which
was nearing the end of its tether.

Like my first over-ambitious and unpublishable novel *Strange
Vista* of ten years before, *High Horse Riderless* was written
compulsively from the desire to clarify and codify my own
ideas rather than with any thought of publication. When the
book was finished it joined *A Painted Ship* in that suitcase under
our bed – but not for long.

In one of his letters, Massingham asked why I did not write
something about the canals. My reply, that I had already done

so but that the result had gone the round of the publishing world in vain, brought a request to see the manuscript. So I dusted it off and dispatched it to him, though without any sense of expectation. A week later came a letter so enthusiastic that it made me realize how badly I had needed the tonic of encouragement. Could he, Massingham asked, send it on to his friend Douglas Jerrold of Eyre & Spottiswoode? Indeed he could, and soon I received an equally encouraging letter from Jerrold accepting the book. A contract followed in September 1943.

Only a fellow author can understand the jubilation a writer feels when his first book is accepted, particularly when that book has such a dreary record of hope deferred. I read through that contract over and over again to assure myself that it was really true. It was as though I had received an unexpected legacy from an unknown rich uncle. Yes, there was my name at the top (hereinafter called the Author) and, believe it or not, the Publishers did 'undertake to produce and publish a work at present entitled *A Painted Ship* at their own risk and expense'. Nor was there any attempt to take advantage of a 'prentice writer's natural desire to get into print. The terms were indeed extremely fair – very much fairer than many a contract I have had to haggle over since. There was only one disappointment. Eyre & Spottiswoode decided not to use the splendid set of photographs that Angela had taken especially to illustrate the book. They evidently classified *A Painted Ship* as a 'country book' and there was – and to some extent still is – a publishing convention that all books of this kind, if illustrated at all, should be illustrated in black-and-white by an artist. I think the theory must be that the cool objective eye of the camera is insufficiently 'romantic' to suit a hey-nonny-no, under-the-greenwood-tree type of text; if so, I think it was a pity to apply this to *A Painted Ship* which was not intended to be that kind of book at all. Its purpose was to make a personal record of the canals and their life which, in the words Massingham used in his Foreword, 'were perishing under the brutal impact of industrialism'. For this reason I wanted photographs to state unequivocally 'this was how it was'. All this must sound uncomplimentary to Denys Watkins-

Pitchford who was commissioned by the publishers to illustrate the book. His scraper-board pictures, most of which were based upon Angela's photographs, have been rightly praised but, however accurate and skilful they may be, it is impossible to rid this type of illustration from the suspicion of romanticism or 'artist's licence'.

I was somewhat mollified when the publishers accepted my suggestion that I should ask my friend Herbert Tooley of the Banbury Boat Dock, who had decorated *Cressy* with the traditional roses and castles so beloved of the boaters, to design a jacket for the book. The result, painted on a wooden panel, was one of the most original and beautiful designs ever to grace a book. It was a tragedy when eventually the block was broken and subsequent editions were no longer able to wear this brave and beautiful thing.

By the time I commissioned Herbert Tooley I had decided upon a change of title. There was something slightly arty-crafty about *A Painted Ship*, I felt. I had also come to the conclusion that a book's title should never be lifted from a poem unless the theme of that poem is relevant to the subject of the book. It certainly could not be said that the horrific story told by Coleridge's Ancient Mariner had anything whatever to do with the English canals, so I re-titled the book, very simply, *Narrow Boat*. The publishers accepted this change with some reluctance, arguing that the term would be meaningless because most people thought of all canal craft as barges.

Six months after *Narrow Boat* was contracted for, my morale received a second fillip. Massingham, for whose literary sponsorship I shall always be grateful, wrote to say that Robert Hale, the publisher, was planning a new series of books on the English counties and that he had recommended me as a likely contributor to his friend Brian Vesey-FitzGerald, who had been appointed general editor of the series. Almost immediately came a letter from Vesey-FitzGerald offering me a choice of three counties; one of them was Worcestershire which I chose without hesitation. Back came a contract from Robert Hale dated March 1944. I had won my first commission.

It was only later that I realized what a remarkable transaction this was. I was completely unknown and with only one book, as yet unpublished, to my credit. Yet I was not asked for any specimen chapter or even for a synopsis. Nor was there any preliminary meeting with editor or publisher. Brian Vesey-FitzGerald did not lay down any guide-lines whatever but gave me a completely free hand. Even the length of the book was elastic – anything from 70,000 to 120,000 words. Although I welcomed such a liberal attitude, I think it was the reason why, when the series eventually appeared, it was decidedly uneven in quality. Authors felt free to mount each his particular hobby horse and ride furiously away for chapter after chapter.

I was not a native of Worcestershire; in fact, I had never even lived in the county until we had moored *Cressy* at Tardebigge in 1941. But there were two reasons for my choice. The first was the purely practical one that, at a time when travel was still severely restricted, my work for the Ministry of Supply gave me a splendid opportunity to kill two birds with one stone by gathering material for the book while travelling round on my job. After all, as a result of such travelling, I already knew a great deal more about Worcestershire than I did when we had first sailed into it three years before. My second reason was that Worcestershire seemed, almost more than any other shire, to represent a microcosm of England both in its social history and in the variety of its topography. Extending northward to embrace Dudley in the Black Country, eastward to the foot of the Cotswold scarp and westward through the Teme valley gap almost to the Marches of Wales, its boundary embraced an immense and meaningful variety of landscape both natural and man-made.

I had always disliked those romanticized books about rural England designed to suppress ugly truths and to make their readers forget that there had ever been an Industrial Revolution or even any Enclosure Acts, by painting a false picture of a countryside unchanged since the Middle Ages, or certainly since the mid-eighteenth century. In this topographical dreamworld such facts of life as factories, housing estates, overhead power lines, railways, or even canals, did not exist. Such

books are the literary equivalent of those photographs of olde
worlde, picturesque villages taken early on a summer morning
before any cars are parked around and from which the wirescape
has been carefully touched out. Their writers make much
play with the adjective 'unspoiled' without pausing to con-
sider its significance, much less to ask themselves who has
done the spoiling and why. I was determined that *Worcestershire*
should not be a book of this genre but should present an honest
portrait of the shire, warts and all, the black Worcestershire
as well as the green. Having just finished *High Horse Riderless*,
this commission seemed a heaven-sent opportunity to write a
case-history illustrating the validity of the general arguments
I had advanced in the earlier book. I would make two journeys
through the shire, one through time and one through space;
taken together, they would demonstrate the interdependence
between man and nature by revealing man's influence, good
and bad, upon the landscape and how, in turn, he had been
influenced by it. So, in my introduction to *Worcestershire*, I
wrote: 'If a topographer sets out to write about his chosen
region something of more moment than a mere guidebook, or
a record of a sentimental journey, he must approach and judge
his subject from some particular standpoint. The standpoint I
have chosen has been the ecological one.' But I very much
doubt whether, at that time, more than one in a hundred readers
knew what I meant by ecology.

Gathering material for this book was a fascinating and
memorable experience. At the time I found it exciting and
rewarding, such was the infinite variety and richness of the
Worcestershire characters to whom it introduced me: Squire
of Stourbridge making fireclay glass-pots by a method which
pre-dated the invention of the potter's wheel; Weaver of
Catshill, last of the Bromsgrove nailmasters, working the
oliver in his back-yard nail forge; Birch of Bewdley, last of the
Wyre Forest broom-squires making his besoms, whisks and
skep baskets; Eddie Moore, the scythe-maker, plating scythe
blades under his water-powered tilt hammer in a little forge
at Bell End; a remarkable old man named George 'Aurelius'
Marcuis, last of a long line of Bewdley river men and barge-
masters; William Fowkes of Droitwich, silver-haired and

soft-voiced, a master furniture maker if ever there was one. Fowkes, in particular, became a dear friend of mine. After a day spent in the offices and machine shops of large factories spewing out weapons of mechanized warfare, what a relief it was to climb the outside wooden stair to his loft workshop and, leaning against a corner of the bench, to talk to this gentle, wise and humble man while he worked, handling his simple tools with a precision marvellously deft. I saw such men as the last representatives of an older social order which, like the natural world, owed its stability to its diversity. In this it was the precise opposite of the society created by modern technology which, driven forward at headlong pace by false economics, is not only chronically unstable, but imposes the shoddy uniformity of the worthless and the second-rate, thus running counter to the needs of human nature and oversetting the delicate balance of the natural world – or the natural order, as I called it at this time.

One of my greatest sources of inspiration was the collection of Worcestershire 'by-gones' with which J. F. Parker and his wife had filled their house at Tickenhill, perched on a hilltop looking down on Bewdley. They had begun by collecting relics of the life and the manifold trades and crafts of that ancient river port, but had gradually expended their range until it covered the whole county. To visit Tickenhill and to take tea before the wood fire, which, in recollection, seemed to blaze perpetually in the open hearth of the great hall, surrounded by such treasure trove was a magical experience. It was utterly unlike any museum. Here were no dead objects, embalmed behind glass and self-consciously displayed; but a treasure house, an Aladdin's cave in which the infinitely varied riches of the past seemed to have acquired a strange new life through the knowledge, understanding and boundless enthusiasm of one elderly, white-haired couple. They proved a powerful source of inspiration where *Worcestershire* was concerned.

I sought out not only Worcestershire's individual craftsmen but also those industries peculiar to the region which had developed from older craft trades: Stourbridge glass workers, Redditch needle makers and the chain-makers of Cradley Heath.

In doing so I made some astonishing discoveries. I shall not forget my amazement on seeing in the barn of a farm near a fireclay mine outside Stourbridge, a small and elderly beam engine, supplied with steam by an old egg-ended boiler, driving a chaff cutter*. With the history of the canals and railways of the county I had long been familiar, but I spent a memorable morning on the footplate of No. 2290, the celebrated ten-wheels-coupled 'Lickey Banker', a labouring giant which spent a long lifetime pushing heavy trains up the 1 in 37 Lickey incline from Bromsgrove to Blackwell. How often of a night time as we lay in bed on *Cressy* did we hear the distant sound of her deep organ-pipe whistle speaking to the train engines, 'I am here and ready', a signal soon to be followed by the slow, syncopated rhythm of steam locomotives labouring heavily in full gear. At such times I would imagine I heard the clang and rattle of the fireman's shovels and see in the mind's eye the intermittent glare from opened fire doors, shining on steam and smoke.

In the first, historical, part of the book I paid tribute to the example of the monastic orders in Worcestershire, both as agriculturists and as founders of craft trades. It seemed to me that the history of these religious communities displayed an intuitive understanding of, and reverence for, the natural order which was summed up in the phrase *Laborare est orare*. Massingham shared this view. We both felt that, although they had been to some extent corrupted by their own worldly success, the dissolution of the monasteries was an almost unmitigated disaster for England. Consequently, because it was the modern custodian of the monastic principles which we so much admired, we both carried on at this time what I can only describe as an uneasy flirtation with the Roman Catholic church.

By what was surely a somewhat remarkable compromise, Massingham was eventually received into that church, but as a non-practising member; the liberal family tradition he inherited would never permit him to swallow the authoritarian dogma of papal infallibility. As he wrote in his autobiography *Remembrance*: 'The abrogation of private judgement is to me an impenetrable wall dividing me from the full Christian

* The engine is now in the Birmingham Museum of Science and Industry.

77

communion.' So whole-heartedly do I agree with this last statement that I do not think I could ever have struck even such an uneasy compromise. As it was, my flirtation with what my father always dismissed with a snort as 'popery' very soon cooled over the mundane but vital question of birth-control.

Birth-control seemed to me an unwarrantable interference with that 'natural order' whose virtues I proclaimed. Yet advances in medical science had already achieved a form of death-control by greatly prolonging man's expectation of life. Consequently, although at this time it was widely held that the population of England would decline after the war, I foresaw an inevitable population explosion which would subject the delicate balance of the natural order to such pressures that it must inevitably lead to a catastrophic breakdown. I had deliberately avoided mentioning this dilemma in *High Horse Riderless* because it seemed the one loose thread in an otherwise satisfactory fabric. I cudgelled my brains over it in vain for many months and finally resolved to write to a noted Jesuit apologist at Farm Street and find out what he had to say on the subject. He replied as follows:

> I think that the answer of the catholic non-technician must be that the end can't justify the means: that however useful a thing may be you can't do it if it's wrong in itself. But that of course isn't helpful. I should have thought that scientific agriculture etc might provide some sort of solution: I've read somewhere about ways of producing plants in tiers for instance, and that sort of thing . . . In fact of course I suppose we have to reckon with the effect of wars and other disasters if we take a factual view . . .

I found this reply so profoundly unhelpful and thought it revealed such shortsightedness, such vagueness and muddled thinking, that it effectually ended my brief flirtation with Catholicism. What struck me as bitterly ironical was that my correspondent should rely on wars and disasters, or on those modern high-priests, the scientists, who, by monoculture, poison sprays and machines, were destroying the natural order and laying waste the earth, to come to his rescue and solve the problem. It seemed to me that it would have been at once more honest and more logical if he had argued that men should not strive to prolong life. In other words, if you argued against birth-control you should take a similar stand against death-control too on the ground that both represented an unwarrantable interference with the natural order. This might seem to be an impossible *reductio ad absurdum;* yet was the suggestion that men should be left to die in their beds any more callous than the priest's own argument that millions might be massacred by modern methods of warfare?

I eventually reasoned that the answer lay in that same 'abrogation of private judgement' that had proved such a stumbling block to Massingham. For what was that abrogation if it was not a denial of man's unique and perilous gift of free-will? This gave to man alone of all species the choice of either recognizing and working with the natural order or flouting it at his peril. To say that men had been divinely ordered to breed like rabbits and then to rely hopefully on war, pestilence or famine to restore the ecological balance seemed to me to assume that man was no better than an animal. Expressed in religious terms, it was a blasphemous denial of a God-given gift. I therefore saw the principle of birth-control as part of man's conscious recognition of a natural order and his willingness to work for it. The alternative spelled chaos and disaster. So, to my own satisfaction at any rate, I solved this nagging problem but at the price of rejecting contemporary Catholic orthodoxy.

Soon after I had been commissioned to write the book on Worcestershire I received a letter from Henry Cornelius, a film producer from South Africa who had come over to this country to make a series of films for Ealing Studios of which the best-known was to be *Genevieve.* He was contemplating a film about the canals and asked whether I could advise him. How he had heard of me I cannot now remember. *Narrow Boat* had not been published, but I had written a number of articles about canals, advocating their greater use, and I can only assume that he must have come across one of these. The upshot of this correspondence was that Cornelius, accompanied by his director, Charles Crichton, came to visit us at Tardebigge, picking their way along the muddy path to the boat one cold day in earliest spring. 'Corney' was a fat and physically unprepossessing South African Jew, but I remember him with affection – he died in the 1950s. He was a strangely endearing and unconventional figure with a remarkably quick and astute mind. On reaching *Cressy* he climbed ponderously aboard, wrapped in an enormous overcoat, removed his pathetically sodden London shoes on the fore-deck, squeezed through the cabin doors and padded into the boat like some large bear. I can see him now as he filled one of our easy chairs before the open stove, twiddling his toes and still huddled in his overcoat. For he had not long arrived from Africa and disliked the English climate.

He was contemplating, he said, making a film about the English canals that would be partly fictional and partly a documentary. I think I must have told him the original title of my book, for he decided to call this film *Painted Boats* and the outcome of this first encounter was that I agreed to act as his technical adviser. I welcomed this opportunity, not because I was dazzled by the world of the movies – we hardly ever went to the cinema – but simply because it promised an entirely new and novel experience. He gave me an outline of the fictional part of the film and its requirements, which included a tunnel, and asked me to advise him as to the best location – preferably not too far from London. I suggested the stretch of the Grand Union canal between Stoke Bruerne and Braunston and this part of the picture was made there, although I was unable to see any of the shooting because my work for the Ministry of Supply prevented it. I introduced 'Corney' to Mr Patterson, the elderly managing director of the Samuel Barlow Coal Company of Birmingham, owners of the Braunston Boatyard, who agreed to the use of Barlow boats in the film. Because all Barlow boats were beautifully painted and turned out by my old friend Frank Nurser of Braunston, I judged that they would look splendid on film. They would have looked even better had the film been made in colour which, at this time, alas, was out of the question. For the purpose of the film, one Barlow butty boat was repainted and re-named *Sunny Valley*. Rather a stupid and uncharacteristic name, I thought privately, but the boat retained it to the end of her working life. Some time after

Sunny Valley's film career was over, Barbara Jones painted her picture as she lay in the covered dock at Braunston, and because I thought this the finest record ever made of a narrow boat in all her glory, I reproduced it subsequently on the jacket and as a frontispiece for my book *Inland Waterways of England*. A full-sized studio mock-up of the cabin and stern-end of *Sunny Valley* was made for the film and this is now displayed in the Waterways Museum at Stoke Bruerne.

I paid several visits to Ealing, first for script conferences and later to see the rushes, at a time when the V1s were droning over London like sinister maybugs. After the conferences were over I was free to wander round the mad, make-believe world of the studios where, with infinite pains, totally unreal simulations of reality were constructed, fit food for those who desired to escape from harsh reality for a while into a world of celluloid fantasy. In one studio they were filming some comedy set in ancient Rome and, lurking behind a seemingly substantial column of plywood and plaster to keep out of camera, I watched them filming over and over again one short sequence lasting not more than a minute and involving two lines of dialogue. I must have watched at least six takes before I became bored and tip-toed away. Those who hanker for the glamour of the movies and those rare mortals who act in them must realize in their saner moments what a tinsel world it is. But what they cannot know is the sheer tedium and frustration of film-making. This illusory reality is as fragile as a soap bubble; the smallest untoward incident, an uncontrollable sneeze, the fusing of a spot or the mechanical failure of a camera to traverse or pan at precisely the right moment and all must be set up again until the nerves of director, actors and camera crews become frayed to exasperation. On location the situation is even worse, for the natural world is seldom cooperative; clouds obscure the sun, rain falls, or a sudden playful wind ruffles the stars and booms in the microphones.

I thought the happiest and most placid man at Ealing Studios, and the only person I envied, was the model-maker. He lurked, like William Fowkes, in a little loft workshop reached by an outside stair. To meet the exacting demands of the film-makers called for boundless ingenuity and powers of invention. This

mild, middle-aged man showed me with pride a beautiful model
of a Spitfire he had just completed for some film about the
R.A.F. It did not have to fly, he had been told, but it had to
show flashes from its wing cannons. He showed me how he had
solved this problem: acetylene gas piped to the wings from a
cylinder in the fuselage. A small battery and electric motor,
also in the fuselage, actuated the gas valves and the ignition
system. But even he must have felt frustrated when the products
of so much thought and craftsmanship were soon cast aside,
assuming they had not been destroyed in the making of the
picture. I saw a large and beautiful model of a ship he had
earlier made for the film *San Demetrio, London* which had then
just been completed. This miniature *San Demetrio*, perfect in
every detail, had now been reduced to a burned and blackened
hulk, forlornly floating in the studio tank.

For the industrial documentary sequences of *Painted Boats* I
had selected five locations on the Birmingham Canals in the
Black Country. At that time the system was busy with horse-
drawn 'day-boats' as well as occasional long-distance pairs of
narrow boats, so there was no need to simulate the action. We
met at the 'Queens Hotel' in Birmingham early one chilly
October morning, Cornelius, Crichton, myself and Douglas
Slocombe, the cameraman. I had warned 'Corny' that bright
light in the Black Country in October was about as rare as
snow on the equator, but film producers seem to be incurably
optimistic. As it happened, we were fortunate, for as we drove
out of Birmingham towards Smethwick a pallid morning sun
was breaking through the mist and murk. But all day it played
a coy game of hide and seek with us, retreating behind some
infuriatingly slow-moving cloud whenever Slocombe was about
to shoot, but shining brightly while we were moving on to
another location. Tempers became frayed. Looking down from
a bridge high above the Tame Valley canal, a long straight
pound stretched away into the distance, its still water looking
like a strip of tarnished silver. Far below us a horse-drawn
day-boat was approaching, lazy ripples fanning out from her
bows. The black shapes of more boats could be seen in the
distance. 'Corney' stamped about on the bridge, shoulders
hunched and hands thrust deep in his overcoat pockets. 'For

Christ's sake shoot it man!' he exclaimed in sudden exasperation. But, shaking his head, Slocombe continued to peer at the
sun through his smoked glass and replied acidly, 'If these
pictures look as if they were taken through pea soup, it won't
be *you* who'll have to carry the can.' And so it went on. But, at
the end of a long day, all the shots had been taken and they
turned out to be an excellent record of still living waterways.

At 'Corney's' suggestion, I wrote the text of a commentary
to accompany the documentary sequences but, to my disappointment, it was rejected. Before film and sound-track had been
married together, the commentary was played over while the
film was shown in the studio cinema. I felt very dashed when,
as the lights came on, Cavalcanti, who was the great panjandrum
at Ealing in those days, threw up his hands and, exclaiming
'No, no, no! It will not do,' walked out. Louis MacNeice was
thereupon commissioned to write another commentary. I hesi-
tate to criticize because it may sound like sour grapes and a
reflection on a dead poet whose work I greatly admire. Nevertheless, I found the result strangely unsatisfactory. It struck me
as too self-consciously 'arty' to fit a simple subject which asked
for equally simple and down-to-earth comment. Most of the
critics spoke well of MacNeice's commentary, but the film critic
of the *Observer* evidently agreed with me. Of the tunnel sequence
he wrote: 'It is always exciting to come out of close darkness
into strong sunlight, and if the moment is well photographed,
it does not require a snatch of modern verse in words of one
syllable to heighten the experience. "Must be, must be, must
be done" drones the sound track, as the prow of the painted
boat slides out into the open.'

At the end of September 1945, Angela and I, accompanied
by Patterson of Samuel Barlow's, attended the trade showing
of *Painted Boats* in a Birmingham cinema. We thought it pretty
good – at least our practised eyes could detect no glaring errors.
But I was somewhat chagrined to find that, after all my labours,
I had not been given a screen credit. It was probably my fault
for not insisting on it in the first place, but I was then totally
unfamiliar with the ways of the film world. In the foyer of the
cinema, Patterson introduced us to a strange dark-haired young
woman. She was wearing flat-heeled open sandals, a blue

peasant skirt of mid-calf length held up by a broad leather belt, and a tight bright yellow jersey. A copy of the *New Statesman* was tucked under her arm. Her name was Sonia South. She had been an actress before the war, whispered Patterson, but had come on to the canals as one of the 'Idle Women'. Now, he added, with a shake of the head, she was just about to marry one of his boatmen. I thought she looked a rather frightening left-wing blue-stocking, and if Patterson had added that this girl would one day become my second wife I would have thought he had taken leave of his senses.

By this time *Narrow Boat* had been published. It first burst upon the world in early December, 1944, and no one was more astonished than I by the reception it received. Not only were there long rave reviews in all the papers, but I was inundated with fan mail which went on arriving for months after publication. I had never expected anything like this. I realized that one of the many unpaid chores that the luckless author is expected to perform is replying to readers' letters. I remembered guiltily that I had never given this problem a thought when I had written to Massingham, but I learnt the lesson now that I was at the receiving end. In case this sounds ungracious let me say at once that some fan letters are charming, a delight to receive and a pleasure to answer. But the student who is writing a thesis and wants to pick my brains; the nigglers who delight to air their superior knowledge by picking on some point of detail ('I would point out that 21st January 1802 was not a Sunday but a Monday'); their letters are not so welcome. The frustrating thing was that the book rapidly went out of print and could not be reprinted because Eyre & Spottiswoode had exhausted their war-time paper quota. However, after an interval of a few months, it appeared again and it has remained in print ever since.

It is no false modesty to say that I cannot altogether account for the success of *Narrow Boat*. Turning back to it now after nearly thirty years I find it too self-consciously arcadian and picaresque. In this it was not strictly truthful. As the first chapter of this book reveals, owing to the outbreak of war, the journey it describes was not really roses, roses all the way. I find it all slightly embarrassing now, and believe its instantaneous popularity was due to the fact that it appeared at precisely the right moment. After four years of war it satisfied a thirst for what is called escapist literature.

It is a handicap to an author to score a success with his first book. After I had published several books, I found it discouraging, on being introduced to a stranger, still to be greeted with the remark, 'Ah! you're the man who wrote *Narrow Boat.*' Fortunately, I eventually succeeded in writing down *Narrow Boat*, and in an entirely different vein. For another disadvantage of a successful first book, I soon discovered, is that its author, if he is not careful, can become set in one groove. I began to receive flattering letters from publishers, many of whom had originally rejected *Narrow Boat*, all asking me for another canal book. But I decided that if, as I had planned, I was going to earn my living as a writer, I could never hope to do so by writing books about canals alone; it was far too narrow and specialized a row to hoe. I might return to the subject later, I thought, but meanwhile let me try something different. So I brought out the manuscript of *High Horse Riderless* from under our bed and sent it to Eyre & Spottiswoode. Although, curiously, their contract for *Narrow Boat* contained no option clause, I felt in honour bound to offer them my next book. They rejected it, which did not altogether surprise me. So I sent it to Philip Unwin of George Allen & Unwin who had been the first to write to me to suggest another canal book. He promptly accepted it as, I suspect, a sprat to catch a mackerel, for there *was* an option clause in his contract.

With those great Chirico white horses still in mind, I asked a friend of mine, Toni del Renzio, a surrealist painter and writer, if he would design a jacket for the book. The result was striking but the horse was quite unlike anything I had expected. In fact it was quite unlike a horse at all. It looked more like a unicorn, startled at having mislaid its horn. I felt I could not say anything to Toni without upsetting him and, after all, it was a symbolical horse and not a real one, so I sent the design to my publishers. It provoked a serious reply that I found highly diverting. The horse, they pointed out, was anatomically incorrect and, as Lady Wentworth's publishers, they were in a position to know. They went on to suggest that their artist should substitute another horse based on the Darley Arabian. They enclosed photographs of the jacket and of their artist's horse so that the latter could be superimposed. I found the Darley Arabian even less meaningful as a symbol than the original, so it was Toni's hornless unicorn that pranced before a bewildered public at a price of 10*s*. 6*d*. in the spring of 1947.

High Horse Riderless was surprisingly well and widely reviewed. Under the heading 'Freedom to Create', it earned a long three columns from Charles Morgan ('Menander') in the *Sunday Times*, something that would be unthinkable today, certainly for any book of this kind. But the review that pleased and encouraged me most was that in the *Listener* where it was noticed along with a book called *Science, Liberty and Peace* by Aldous Huxley. It began:

> Both Mr. Rolt and Mr. Huxley make precisely the same diagnosis of our ills, and both prescribe precisely the same immediate treatment. So closely, indeed, do they agree that on almost every page of Huxley's shorter essay you can find a passage which can be paralleled from Mr. Rolt's more detailed analysis.

The review went on to prove the point by a series of cross-quotations. Because for ten years Aldous Huxley had been my most admired of all living prose writers, it may be imagined how gratified and honoured I felt to find myself unexpectedly in such august company. It was as though some young and aspiring poet were suddenly to find his work compared with that of W. B. Yeats. The anonymous reviewer was unusually percipient for he wrote: 'Neither author mentions the population question. Surely we want to know how we are to decentralize a population of 766 persons per square mile, which was the figure for England in 1939.'* And he concluded sadly: 'We are not likely to change our ways under pressure of a threat which does not seem imminent.'

A dear and wise friend of mine in the publishing world once remarked to me: 'It's not column-inches of review space that sells books, nor advertising, it's personal recommendation.' In

---

* In fairness to the late Aldous Huxley, it should be said that he became deeply concerned with the population explosion long before such concern became general.

my literary career I have proved the truth of this over and over again. Books which have been virtually ignored by the popular press, and particularly by 'the Sundays', have sold widely and, what is much more important, have gone on selling. With *High Horse Riderless* it was the precise opposite. Its one small first edition slowly sold out and the book was never reprinted, although it did appear in Danish translation. Readers might have an avid appetite for what they regarded as an 'escapist' book about the canals, but the 'great questions', the uncomfortable and disturbing truths, they found unpalatable. The threat did not seem imminent, so they did not want to know.

High Horse Riderless was a pessimistic book written in an optimistic mood. When I wrote it I had felt so certain that there would be a change of heart after the war. But long before it was published the horrors of Belsen and Buchenwald had been revealed, and atomic bombs had been dropped on the cities of Hiroshima and Nagasaki. The news of these events turned my brief optimism to an extreme pessimism that came near to despair.

It was a gloriously warm and sunny day, I remember, and Angela and I had gone walking on the southern end of the Malvern Hills. We sat on the top of Chase End hill among the young bracken fronds and gazed out over the lovely landscape of the Severn vale below us, rimmed by the distant blue wall of the Cotswolds on the skyline. Peace had returned to Europe, the sun was shining out of a cloudless sky and it was good to be alive. It was when we returned in the evening that we heard on the wireless the news that the first atomic bomb had been loosed upon a defenceless city with such appalling results. In an essay which I wrote subsequently* I tried to describe the agony of mind and the sense of despairing impotence that I felt at that moment; it would be true to say that my outlook from that day to this has been profoundly affected by that event. It was as though the evils I had inveighed against in *High Horse Riderless* had suddenly materialized to reveal a hideous strength that exceeded my wildest imaginings. From that day I have never doubted that evil now possessed the power to commit the ultimate blasphemy of destroying all the life and beauty of the

* 'To Gain our Peace' in *The Clouded Mirror* (1955).

world: either by destroying the planet utterly or by transforming it into a poisoned desert peopled by deformed monsters. From now on, all things seemed tragically ephemeral. To typify the state of mind of those who could conceive and perpetrate such unbelievable horrors, in my essay I quoted Milton's prince Lucifer:

> . . . To bow and sue for grace
> With suppliant knee, and deify his pow'r,
> Who from the terror of this arm so late
> Doubted his empire; that were low indeed.

In other words, it was better to reign in hell than serve in heaven, even if that reign spelled ultimate self-destruction. This was some years before the C.N.D. movement got under way and I marvelled that few others appeared to feel as I did. Were they too stunned by such appalling news to react to it? Or were they unwilling to admit its dreadful implications to their consciousness? Perhaps, as the reviewer had said, the threat still did not seem imminent. However, no matter how grave the threat, it was useless to give way to despair; one had to go on living.

With the ending of the war in Europe, my department of the Ministry of Supply was rapidly running down. As I have said, most of my colleagues were temporary civil servants recruited from the engineering industry. Yet now they all began to display a surprising eagerness 'to get on to the establishment'. Perhaps they had learned to prefer the orderly, if dull and ill-paid, routine of a Government department to the industrial rat-race they had known before the war. I do not blame them. I do not know whether they succeeded in their aim or not because I was the first to resign. I was eager to resume the way of life which had been so rudely interrupted by the war – to live on my boat and write for my livelihood. Whether I should have been quite so eager to throw up a secure job had it not been for the unexpected success of *Narrow Boat* I cannot say. Some Government departments, particularly, it seems, the Patent Office, have provided many writers with financial security and a peaceful haven. Yet my craving for freedom and independence was so strong that I believe I would have come to the same decision even if I had not had a word published. To hell with

security! As an earnest of my emancipation, I quickly sold my
official means of transport, that terrible Austin, re-awakened
my faithful old steed, the 1924 'duck's back' Alvis which had
been slumbering in a shed at Stanley Pontlarge, and drove her
triumphantly back to Tardebigge. What a rare pleasure it was
to be at the wheel of a real motor car once more.

Angela had had a brilliant idea. This was that we should
explore by boat the canals and rivers of Ireland – a country
which neither of us had ever visited – and that I should then
write a book about it, a kind of Irish equivalent of *Narrow Boat*
in fact. Obviously *Cressy* could not cross the Irish Sea and we had
some difficulty in locating a suitable craft in Ireland. Eventually
we found *Le Coq*, a ship's lifeboat converted into a small cabin
cruiser, which was lying on the Shannon at Athlone, and agreed
to charter her for three months during the summer of 1946. I
have chronicled this Irish adventure very fully in *Green and
Silver** and it would be superfluous to tell that story again here.
It is enough to say that three months of slow voyaging across
the wide, dark bogs of Ireland's central plain, and over the
broad lakes and reedy reaches of the Shannon, enabled us to get
beneath the skin of that country as no visitor could ordinarily do.
As a result, we fell in love with Ireland and the Irish people;
and though I have been able to return all too seldom since, I
shall always think of Ireland as a second home.

After more than four years lying idly at her moorings at
Tardebigge, our good ship *Cressy* needed docking and repairs.
We therefore planned to return to what we had come to regard
as her home port, Tooley's Boatyard at Banbury, and leave her
there in Herbert Tooley's care while we were away in Ireland.
We hoped, optimistically as things turned out, that repairs
would be completed by the time we returned. So, on 14 April
1946, we 'winded' her in the basin at the New Wharf and, as we
waved farewell to our old friends in the canal workshops,
Cressy slid into Tardebigge tunnel. A landscape that had become
so familiar over four years was suddenly blotted out. As the
darkness swallowed us up, it seemed to me as I stood aft,
getting the feel of *Cressy*'s tiller once again, that it was as
though a camera shutter had suddenly closed on a well-loved

* George Allen & Unwin, 1949.

scene of sunlit brightness. Another long and eventful chapter in my life was ended. The bright disc of light in the darkness that marked the end of the tunnel seemed to symbolize an unknown future. I sighted *Cressy*'s bow on that little golden circle and headed her straight towards it.

Chapter 5

Canal Crusade

Before the war, when I first had the optimistic idea of trying to earn my living as a writer, I had thought of this new career simply as a source of creative satisfaction and as a means of achieving that complete independence and privacy which I had always craved. Strange though it may seem, it had never occurred to me that there was an inescapable corollary to this neat scheme which was the price of its success. Books need readers; I could not make a living by writing the kind of books I wanted to write without publicizing the things I loved and, incidentally, without publicizing myself. In the modern world, even the least dazzling beam of public limelight can prove as lethal as gamma rays, corroding the personality of the 'private man' with the most subtle of poisons. And, like so many poisons, this one is addictive; men seek it as desperately as any drug. It is also isolating, cutting men off from normal, unselfconscious relationships with all except a few most intimate friends. As for writing about well-loved things or places, in our overcrowded island this can be tantamount to giving them the kiss of death. It was the reception of *Narrow Boat* and the shoals of letters I received as a result that first made me realize that there were such unforeseen strings attached to my projected way of earning a living, although it would be hypocritical to say that I was not gratified. Yet I still had no inkling of – and, indeed, had never considered – the possible long-term effect of the book upon its subject, the English canals.

I had known the canals for fifteen years and lived on them for five, and in that time I had come to love them and their people. For me they represented the equivalent of some uncharted, arcadian island inhabited by simple, friendly and unselfconscious natives where I could free myself from all that I found so uncongenial in the modern world. It seems fantastic to me now that when I was writing *Narrow Boat* I did not realize that I was putting this island firmly on the chart. The book was described by one reviewer as 'an elegy of classic restraint'. If it was elegiac it was because I realized that this old and simple world of the canals was too fragile to resist for very long the relentless march of technology captained by modern economic theory. But I certainly never foresaw how very soon the natural life of that world would come to an end. Admittedly, on some canals such as the Worcester & Birmingham, commercial traffic was visibly failing; but on many other narrow canals of the Midlands traffic had increased substantially, so that I saw no reason to suppose that it would so rapidly decline into extinction in the post-war world.

Among the many letters I received following the publication of *Narrow Boat* was one suggesting the formation of a voluntary society ('something like the friends of Canterbury cathedral') to campaign for the greater use of canals and proposing a meeting to discuss the idea further. This letter came from an address in Bloomsbury and was signed Robert Fordyce Aickman. Such a notion had never occurred to me, but anything which might help the canal boaters could not, I thought, fail to be a good thing so I welcomed the idea enthusiastically. Had I not acted so impulsively I might have questioned whether it was such a good idea and so have avoided the storms which lay ahead. But at this time my experience of running voluntary organizations was extremely limited. It was exclusively confined to the Committee of the Vintage Sports Car Club before the war where there had been no clashes of temperament. On the contrary, the atmosphere there had been so harmonious that all the issues discussed were settled by mutual agreement and never had to be put to the vote. I assumed in my innocence that such a happy state of affairs was the rule rather than the exception, but I was to learn otherwise. The launching of the Inland Waterways Association, as we named it, and its promotion, was to become my major preoccupation for the first five

years after the war. But although they were years of considerable
achievement, some of them memorable, they led finally to a
sense of growing frustration and ended in complete exasperation. Now that time has distanced these events I can see that
they had their funny side, so that what appeared then to be a
tragedy appears in retrospect a black comedy. There is certainly
a ludicrous element about our foibles and frailties however
infuriating they may be at the time; nevertheless, there can
be no doubt that our infant Association would have had a much
more healthy childhood had there not been so much bickering
among its parents.

At a preliminary meeting in London at which Robert Aickman
assumed the chair, my old friend Charles Hadfield and I were
elected Vice-Chairman and Honorary Secretary respectively.
Charles Hadfield has since become famous as a canal historian.
He, also, had written to me as a result of *Narrow Boat* and I
was responsible for drawing him in. After this first meeting
I returned to *Cressy* filled with enthusiasm and bashed out on
my typewriter a Constitution and Rules for the new Association,
a booklet, to be illustrated with Angela's photographs, entitled
The Future of the Waterways which set forth our aims, and a
leaflet-cum-entry-form for distribution to likely members.
These three efforts were approved at our next meeting,
although the first two were subsequently destined to be much
revised by another hand. Each of us compiled a list of names
and addresses of possible members to whom the leaflet would
be sent. Mine included all my *Narrow Boat* correspondents, for
I had fortunately kept all their letters which made a formidable
pile.

Because Angela and I had arranged our Irish canal trip before
the new Association was first mooted, I was not in England
but afloat on the Shannon when the new canal crusade was
launched by the sending out of the leaflets in the late spring of
1946. I was told that subscriptions were coming in well; but
coupled with this came the news that Charles Hadfield had
resigned as Vice-Chairman. This was disturbing and saddening
because I had taken an immediate liking to Charles who has
been a very good friend of mine from that day to this. Remote
from the centre of events, I could not then fathom the reason

for his withdrawal, though I realized later that this was only the first ominous cloud in a sky presaging future storms. Charles had acutely sized up a situation that was still not clear to me.

We returned to England and Banbury in September to find that *Cressy* had still not been dry-docked but was lying at her moorings exactly as we had left her three months before. This was tiresome because it was not possible for us to live aboard while she was on the dock. We were forced to hire a caravan which we parked in the boatyard while the work was done, finding it very cramped and inconvenient after our boat. As autumn drew on we also realized that it was very much colder. We appreciated then as never before how effective an insulator water is, for although we turned on heat in that caravan until our heads were bursting, our legs remained obstinately numb from the knees down due to the cold that struck up through the floor. We were back on *Cressy* again by mid-November fortunately, because that winter of 1946–7 turned out to be the longest, coldest and hardest we had ever known. For weeks *Cressy* was locked in ice several inches thick, usually covered with a deep layer of snow, and it was early March before the weather broke with tremendous gales and floods. However, our boat was extremely warm and snug, and in this respect we were a great deal better off than most landsmen during that dismal winter of prolonged power cuts and fuel shortages. But it was a hard time for our friends the boaters, many of whom were frozen in beside us. Most of them found temporary employment with Banbury Corporation, clearing the snow from the streets. Even so, the 'Number Ones' – those who owned their own boats – were forced to draw upon their precious 'docking money', a sum set aside for the repair of their boats. Yet they managed to remain remarkably cheerful and many a pleasant evening we spent with them in the bars of 'The Leather Bottle' or 'The Struggler'; men and women – never together but always separately – dancing to the music of a melodeon that was passed from hand to hand among the boatmen.

'The Struggler' was a small and outwardly insignificant street-corner pub in a back-street which was much frequented by the boaters and also, at fair times, by gypsies and horse-dealers. It had the unusual sign of a globe with a man's legs protruding from one side of it and his head the other. It bore the legend: 'Oh Lord help me through this World'. This used to strike me as singularly appropriate for its roving, impoverished but undaunted customers, none of whom fitted into the neat, organized pattern of modern society. I once described a typical evening spent in 'The Struggler' so I will not do so again.* I did not then name either the pub or the place for obvious reasons. But now there is no further need for such reticence. Developers have destroyed 'The Struggler' and even if they had not, its bar would never again see such a company because the boaters and their boats are all gone. Most of the gypsies and horse-dealers have gone into limbo with them. In the tidy, aseptic world that we have made there is no place for them.

It was not only with the canal boaters and gypsies that I became acquainted during successive winters spent at moorings at Tooley's Yard. I never forgot my first love, railways, and got to know a G.W.R. relief signalman named Billy Bevington. A relief signalman must be prepared, often at short notice, to stand in for any signalman who may happen to be ill or on leave. This meant that Billy had an intimate knowledge of every box on the Paddington–Birmingham main line within cycling distance of Banbury. I used to receive cryptic messages from him such as 'Banbury Junction this week 2 till 10', which meant that he would be pleased to welcome me to that box at any time between those hours. Sometimes on such visits he would sit down in the home-made chair (essential in any signal box) by the stove and leave me to work the block instruments, set the road and 'pull the sticks off'. In this way I gained experience which would eventually become virtually unrepeatable, at any rate on a main line such as this, owing to the installation of modern electrical signalling systems. What impressed me was the strength of tradition on the railways, and also the comparative crudity of the old manual system on which railway safety depended. To illustrate the first point, Billy habitually referred to a stopping train that ran 'all stations' between Birmingham and Oxford as 'the Parly', a name going back to the early days of railways when a Parliamentary Act compelled reluctant

* *Inland Waterways of England* (1950), pp. 183–5.

companies such as the G.W.R. to cater for third-class passengers. As to crudity I vividly remember one Saturday afternoon at Banbury North Box when the signal wire of the down starter parted with a melodious twang as he was 'pulling his sticks off' for a 'runner' (a Paddington–Birmingham non-stop express). Knowing there was no hope of getting a linesman out at such short notice on a Saturday, Billy handed me an old pair of pliers and a coal hammer saying, 'Go down below and see what you can do about it, Tom.' Obediently I passed through the little door beneath the box stairway and threaded my way through a maze of point rods, signal wires, bell cranks and interlocking bars until I had found the broken wire. I never realized until then how extremely tough signal wire is, especially when one has to attack it with totally inadequate tools; the knowledge that time was not on my side did not help matters either. 'Look sharp' called a voice from above as I sweated and struggled. At last I managed to form the two broken ends into rough hooks which, by slacking off the wire adjuster, I managed to link together. 'Try it now,' I called up, 'but for God's sake take it easy.' Fortunately it was only a short pull and to my relief my extempore repair held, the lever swung over into the 'off' position and I emerged from the box to see for myself that the signal arm had obediently dropped. Hardly had I done so than the train, drawn by an immaculate 'Castle' class locomotive, flashed past me with a roar, a brief glimpse of thrashing coupling rods, the echo of a whistle just closed and the swift rhythm of bogie wheels over rail joints. I caught a momentary glimpse of passengers taking tea in the restaurant car and thought wryly that but for my pliers and coal hammer their train would have come to a grinding halt.

At Banbury Junction Box there existed a very curious device in the shape of a hand-cranked dynamo, the purpose of which was to provide power assistance for a set of points a very long way away from the box. The junction concerned was that between the G.W.R. main line and the Great Central Branch from Woodford and the point in question admitted freight trains from off this branch into Banbury hump marshalling yard. Whenever the lever controlling it needed pulling off, Billy would call, 'Wind away, Tom, go on – faster!' The whole

1. Kegworth Top Lock, River Soar, August 1939

2. On a lock gate, Kennet & Avon Canal, early 1930s

3. Wartime mooring at Tardebigge, 1941–6

4. Harry Rogers of Ironbridge

5. Canal campaigning: the Worcester & Birmingham Canal empty and under repair, late 1940s

6. *Cressy* at Lifford bridge, Stratford Canal

7. Mission completed, Lifford bridge

8. *Cressy* leaves the Stratford Canal for the Worcester & Birmingham Canal at King's Norton Stop Lock

9. Ambition achieved, 1949. Crossing Pont Cysyllte with Hugh and Gunde Griffith

10. The long hot summer. Mooring at Vron Cysyllte

11. Duke's Cut, July 1950. The Humphry family about to drop down the back water to Wolvercote Mill

12. Sonia Smith on Warwick on the Grand Union Canal, 1950

13. The author steering Cressy at Hawkesbury Stop, 1950

operation reminded me of one of those children's toys that derives its motion from the energy stored in a heavy flywheel. The principle was exactly the same. But by far the most interesting and unusual signal box in the Banbury area stood close beside the Oxford canal just outside Fenny Compton station. It was islanded between the G.W.R. main line on the one hand and the single line of the S.M.J.,* now part of the L.M.S. system, on the other. It was a 'facing both ways' box with G.W.R. type block instruments and frame on one side and on the other a small L.M.S. frame with its accompanying tablet instruments to control the single line sections.

That bitter first winter at Banbury I was a member of a deputation, led by the late lamented A. P. Herbert (who had agreed to be the Association's President) which had been formed for the purpose of visiting the then Minister of Transport to urge upon him the greater use of canals in the post-war world. I recall this because our appointment was in the morning which meant our catching an early train from Banbury to Paddington. Woken by our alarum clock at a godless hour, we dressed by lamplight in unfamiliar and uncomfortable London clothes and then looked out to see, in the first pale light of dawn, that there had been a fresh and heavy fall of snow in the night which had covered the boat, the frozen canal and the stacks of seasoning oak planks in the boat-yard in a blanket of white eight inches deep. We floundered across the yard to the high wooden gate giving on to Factory Street to find it still padlocked. Instead of climbing it, how much easier, we thought, to walk across the frozen canal to the towpath. I led the way boldly and immediately my left leg went straight through the snow and ice into the canal up to the knee. As luck would have it I had picked the one place in the canal where the ice had been broken the evening before for the purpose of watering a horse. If we were to catch our train there was nothing for it but to press on, so we hurried through the snow to the station, my sodden trouser leg flapping against my shin and canal water squelching inside my shoe. Our hope of finding an empty

* S.M.J. stood officially for Stratford-upon-Avon & Midland Junction but unofficially for Slow, Mouldy & Jolting. The railway along with the box as I knew it has long ago disappeared.

compartment on the train was vain, and our travelling companions were somewhat disconcerted when I removed my shoe and sock and placed them against the radiator under the seat. But for their presence I would have removed my trousers as well. Fortunately there was just time to give them a hurried ironing and pressing before the deputation left for Berkeley Square House. It was all in a good cause, or so we hoped.

When a belated spring eventually arrived, we decided that the time had come to do some campaigning for the new Association by deed instead of merely by word. This was just before the canals were nationalized, and we decided that two of the railway-owned canals, the Stratford and the Welsh Section of the Shropshire Union, should be the targets for our attack. We had learned that the Lifford drawbridge at the northern end of the Stratford Canal, which we had passed under with difficulty on our way to Tardebigge in 1941, had since collapsed under heavy road traffic and that the G.W.R. had replaced it by a 'temporary' fixed steel structure which made the canal impassable by anything larger than a canoe. Unlike the southern end of this canal between its junction with the Grand Union at Kingswood and Stratford-upon-Avon which was then in an advanced state of decay, this northern section had been used in comparatively recent times by commercial traffic trading between London and the south of Birmingham. The trade in cocoa beans and chocolate 'crumb' from London docks to the Cadbury factory at Bournville had been a notable example of such movements, and I then saw no reason why such trade might not be resumed provided the canal could be opened up.

In challenging the might of the G.W.R. we had one trump card to play which has now, most unfortunately, been lost – a statutory right of navigation.* We therefore persuaded Lord

---

* This right was written into most, though not all, of the original canal Acts. The Act for the Derby Canal was one of the exceptions. This enabled the Derby Canal Company to defeat a plot, laid between Brigadier H. E. Hopthrow of I.C.I., Mr Mallender, Managing Director of the Derby Gas, Light & Coke Company and myself to bring a pair of boats laden with coal on to the eastern section of the canal. Somehow the canal company got wind of this scheme and foiled us by the simple expedient of chaining and padlocking the gates of the entrance lock at the junction with the Erewash Canal at Sandiacre. Shortly afterwards the Company applied for and obtained an abandonment order on the grounds that there had been no commercial traffic on their waterway for many years.

Methuen, who was a member of the new Association, to put down a question about Lifford bridge in the House of Lords. It is ironical that after nationalization such a question would have been brushed aside in the House as 'a matter for the day-to-day concern of the transport authority'. In 1947, however, it was quite a different story and it obviously caused quite a stir at Paddington. For the reply was that Lifford bridge would be lifted at any time on notice of an intended passage being given. So we duly gave notice of our intention to pass through the canal on 20 May.

Of this and subsequent voyages I have an accurate record because I continued to keep as complete a log of each day's journeying as I had done on our honeymoon voyage in 1939. I see from this that we slipped our moorings at Banbury on 14 May and moored in the basin at Kingswood on Saturday the 17th. We were surprised to see an empty motor narrow boat, *Bilster*, also moored in this deserted basin and discovered that the G.W.R. had chartered this craft from the Grand Union Canal Company's Hatton Maintenance Depot with the object of putting her through ahead of us to clear a passage and so avert the adverse publicity which might result if *Cressy* got hopelessly stuck or was damaged. The G.W.R. was obviously taking the affair seriously. Already the venture was attracting some attention and the next day's entry in my log reads briefly: 'Sunday, 18th May. Poured practically all day. Lay at Kingswood troubled by reporters and I.W.A. members.' This led me to reflect wryly on the contrast with our previous voyage in 1941 when we had slipped through the canal unnoticed and without any fuss. But I consoled myself with the thought that it was all in a good cause.

The next day dawned fine but cold and overcast. At 10 o'clock the *Bilster* set off up the Lapworth locks with G.W.R. and G.U.C. engineers on board. Knowing that even an empty boat of this type draws more at the stern end than did *Cressy*, from my previous experience of the canal I did not fancy her chances of getting through and my fear was that she might become hopelessly stuck in a bridge-hole and so block the canal for us. I decided to give her a good start, so we did not leave until 2 p.m. The state of the canal had certainly deteriorated since 1941, for although we climbed the nineteen locks without incident, the weed in the long summit pound was so thick that for about a mile in the neighbourhood of Hockley Heath we had to resort to bow-hauling from the overgrown towpath. Then conditions improved somewhat so that we were able to go forward slowly under our own power once more until we tied up for the night beside the junction of the canal feeder channel from Earlswood Lakes.

We had not travelled very far next morning before I saw ahead of us the sight I had most feared – the *Bilster* firmly wedged in a bridge-hole. A number of men were either pulling or shoving without result, and though we added our weight to theirs, still she would not budge, being obviously hard aground on a mound of debris. From the other side of the high towpath hedge came the unmistakable sound of a Fordson tractor at plough, and we succeeded in persuading its driver to unhitch it and drive it on to the towpath. Quite how this difficult man-oeuvre was achieved I cannot now remember. For, as anyone familiar with canals will know, there are no gateways between fields and canal towpaths as local farmers and landowners had no desire to provide free pasturage for boatmen's horses. However, I have a press photograph to prove that this feat was achieved, whereupon the Fordson successfully pulled *Bilster* through the bridge. We then followed suit, man-handling *Cressy* as I was not going to risk a broken propeller.

We had hardly got fairly under way once more before, on round-ing a bend, we saw *Bilster* once again, not stuck in a bridge-hole this time but aground in the middle of the canal. The only thing to be done was to try and edge *Cressy* past, and no one was more surprised than I was when this manoeuvre succeeded. Moreover, when alongside I was able to pass a line over *Bilster*'s fore-end stud and make it fast, which successfully pulled her off. I now had this official 'trail-blazer' in tow, a somewhat humiliating situation for her charterers though it proved to be short-lived. As we approached the next bridge-hole I stopped my propeller as a precaution and sure enough we grounded at the stern. Although we managed to haul her over the obstruction without much difficulty it was obvious that the *Bilster* would be in worse trouble here than ever before. Her captain had obviously weighed up the situation and had come to the same conclusion, for he signalled me to cast off the tow and leave him to his fate. What the end of his story was we never knew, for that was the last we saw of the *Bilster*.

We went ahead very slowly and cautiously. There was always in my mind the fear that *Cressy* might hit some under-water obstruction, 'knock a bottom up' and sink ignominiously and expensively in the middle of the canal. The thought of those muddy waters slowly rising over the floor of our carpeted saloon and up the spines of the lowest bookshelf was a nightmare prospect on which I did not care to dwell. Indeed this whole venture was rather like taking a long-cherished old family motor car on some tough, chassis-breaking reliability trial. But at last we reached King's Norton tunnel without untoward incident, and soon after we had emerged from its darkness the infamous Lifford 'drawbridge' appeared ahead. Unlike the previous occasion when we had passed this way, it presented an animated scene. The steel decking which had replaced the old wooden bridge had been jacked up on to wooden packing by a posse of overalled G.W.R. gangers who were standing by, and the towpath was lined with spectators, mostly press reporters and photographers. The gang had evidently decided to do no more work on their jacks than was absolutely necessary, for there were only a couple of inches to spare over our roof tank as *Cressy* was slowly manhandled beneath the girders. I remembered the shoal beyond the bridge on which *Cressy* had grounded heavily on the previous occasion. It consisted of ashes ejected from the boiler house of a factory beside the towpath, and we soon found that it had grown in the five years that had since elapsed. But at least there was no lack of manpower this time. Normally, I dislike spectators when engaged upon exploits of this kind, but there are occasions when they can be useful and this was one of them. If the last hundred yards of canal to the junction stop lock had been completely dry, I think sheer enthusiasm would have dragged us there. Nevertheless, after the crowds and the questioning, it was a relief to plunge like a rabbit into a burrow into the dark depths of West Hill tunnel and so escape from it all. We were on our own again.

This episode was only the opening chapter in the saga of

Lifford bridge, for had we allowed matters to rest there is no doubt at all that the status quo would have remained undisturbed. Somehow, we had to ensure a series of repeat performances until it dawned on the canal owners (soon to be the British Transport Commission) that it might be cheaper to reconstruct the bridge than continually to send large gangs of men to jack it up. So we begged all members of our infant association to take their boats through the Stratford Canal, but unfortunately the number of members with suitable boats was in those days very small. One of this minority who had a go was Peter Scott. He had a narrow boat converted by a boatyard in Birmingham with the object that, when moored on the Gloucester & Berkeley Ship Canal, she would form a convenient hostel for students visiting his then newly formed Wildfowl Trust at Slimbridge. This boat, the *Beatrice*, followed the design of *Cressy* very closely, even to the paintwork and the fitting of a Model 'T' Ford engine. The only difference was that this engine drove a small propeller directly instead of copying Kyrle Willans's arrangement of reduction drive to a large propeller. This proved to be mistaken, for putting *Beatrice* full astern had no effect whatever on her forward progress, the little propeller being about as much use as an egg whisk.

When *Beatrice* was ready to make her maiden voyage from Birmingham to Slimbridge, instead of going by the direct route, Peter dutifully took her down to Kingswood and thence through the Stratford Canal. On this occasion I joined *Beatrice* on the Lapworth Locks and my voyage as 'pilot' was made ever memorable, not by any untoward occurrence on the Stratford Canal but by an episode in West Hill tunnel. We had just about reached the middle of this long tunnel when I heard the engine die, the ensuing silence broken only by an echoing exclamation from Peter who was at the tiller. I hurried aft and soon discovered the cause of the trouble. He had grossly underestimated *Beatrice*'s thirst for fuel. Her fuel tank was completely dry, nor had anyone thought to lay on any spare cans. There was nothing for it but to manhandle the boat out of the tunnel.

The Worcester & Birmingham Canal was, I think, unique among the old canal companies in possessing its own telephone system throughout. Although this had long ago fallen into disuse, the metal brackets that had carried the insulators still existed along the crown of the tunnel roof. By standing on the cabin, pushing against each bracket in turn while I walked aft and then running for'ard to wait for the next bracket to come up, I found I could keep the boat moving at about half its normal speed. By the time we finally emerged from the south end of the tunnel, dusk was falling and I was not only exhausted but black as a sweep from the accumulation of soot that the vanished steam tug *Droitwich* had left on the tunnel roof. It was noticeable that the other I.W.A. members present on this occasion took no part in these proceedings but remained below drinking tea, content to leave it to Peter and myself to extricate them from this predicament. I have never 'legged' a boat through a canal tunnel in the traditional manner, but this experience was the next best thing and gave me a very fair idea of the sheer physical effort involved despite the fact that *Beatrice* was only the equivalent of a half-empty boat.

My 1947 assault on the Stratford Canal was only the first stage of a much more ambitious and venturesome voyage. Ever since I had experienced her first steam trials on the Welsh Canal in 1929, I had determined that one day I would pilot *Cressy* over Telford's great aqueduct across the Vale of Llangollen at Pont Cysyllte. Ten years later I had been foiled in the attempt by the outbreak of war, and now I was going to try again. In the meantime, however, the outcome of this venture had become very much more uncertain. No boats had voyaged from Hurleston Junction to Llangollen since before the war and, what was more, in 1944 the L.M. & S.R. had obtained Parliamentary powers which enabled the company to abandon the entire canal. Boats were permitted to enter it on sufferance, but the 1944 Act had extinguished the right of navigation. This meant that if *Cressy* sank, became hopelessly stuck or encountered an obstruction like Lifford bridge, I could obtain no legal redress, nor could I invoke any aid from the company. Once past Hurleston Junction, where the canal joins the main line of the Shropshire Union Canal, it would literally become a case of sink or swim.

After a short stay in brilliantly fine weather on our old moorings at Tardebigge, we locked down the famous 'thirty and twelve' en route for Worcester and the river Severn. At Diglis, Worcester, we swung right-handed on to the river and headed upstream in the direction of Stourport. At that time some friends of ours were living at Shrawley Wood House which lies close beside the west bank of the Severn just below Stourport. They joined us at Worcester, the idea being that, after luncheon on board, they would travel with us as far as Shrawley where we would moor up for the night so that they could entertain us to dinner. This had seemed an excellent idea, but it proved singularly difficult to carry out as anyone familiar with the high and thickly overgrown banks of the Severn will appreciate. The tremendous wash created by the many tanker barges that were then using the river added to the hazards of such an uncongenial mooring. Nevertheless we contrived to moor eventually beside the mouth of the Dick brook, and in this way I discovered the mysterious ruins of the mason's lock chambers built by Andrew Yarranton when he made the brook navigable in 1652. The course of the brook is so narrow and tortuous, the lock (or half-lock?) chambers so large and massive, that the whole set-up was a profound puzzle to me then as it still puzzles industrial archaeologists today.

Happily no harm came to *Cressy* at her somewhat risky mooring, and next morning we were soon locking up through the two large locks at Stourport which link the Severn with the terminal basin of the Staffordshire & Worcestershire Canal. We now intended to follow this as far as its junction with the 'main line' of the Shropshire Union at Autherley. This particular length of canal carried a very heavy traffic that was almost entirely horse drawn, for the power station at Stourport then took the bulk of its coal by water from the Cannock coalfield. This traffic was worked exclusively by what the long distance canal boaters used to call, not without a certain disdain, 'Joey boat-men' – men who crewed the short-haul 'day-boats' peculiar to the canal system of the Black Country. More crudely built than the long distance craft, the diminutive cabins of these day-boats were never used as homes but only as shelters for the crew of two during the day. The 'turn' from Gailey to Stourport was the longest to be worked by such craft and it was organized in two shifts, one gang working the boats between Gailey and the

'Stewponey Inn' where they handed over a loaded boat to their mates for the remainder of the journey, picking up an empty boat for the return journey.

We also saw on this canal a very significant relic of the canal past. This was the *Symbol*, an old Shropshire Union Canal Carrying Company horse-drawn fly-boat. She was now drably painted and bore the letters 'L.M. & S.R.' on her cabin sides, but her graceful lines and the fact that her name was carved on her stern made her origin unmistakable. Worked by two men, she was carrying general cargo and assorted parcels – the sort of traffic that once travelled 'fly' – between an L.M.S. Canal depot in the Black Country and Stourport. The *Symbol* was thus an inexplicable survivor of the long defunct Shropshire Union Canal Carrying Company. With the coming of nationalization it quickly vanished; why such a traffic movement had survived for so long it is hard to say. Competition between rival railway companies is probably the answer.

Although it was obvious that the *Symbol* was an anachronism, the traffic in coal to Stourport power station seemed such a logical movement that we had no doubts about its future. Evidently the newly appointed Docks & Inland Waterways Executive had no doubts either, for one of its first acts after nationalization was to dredge the whole canal between Gailey and Stourport. Hardly had this costly exercise been completed when the National Coal Board and the Central Electricity Generating Board agreed between them that future supplies of coal to Stourport should go by rail or road, and the coal drops beside the canal at Gailey were promptly demolished. This was a typical example of the follies that so soon followed upon nationalization, and it explains why our experience in 1947 was so soon to become a part of history. To see a wide and dusty towing path trampled by the hoof prints of many horses, to smell horse dung and to see the 'eloquent grooves' worn in metal rubbing strips by innumerable tow lines still bright from constant use, such trifles, once so commonplace in the canals, were never to be experienced again. Next year, when we passed that way, the traffic had vanished; weeds were already encroaching on the disused towpath, and the bright rope grooves had grown dull.

Our journey up the main line of the Shropshire Union from Autherley Junction was uneventful and we arrived at Nantwich to find that the entrance to the basin had been dredged out since our previous visit; so, to our relief, we were able to find a good mooring in the basin. It was here we learnt that we were to have company on our voyage up the Welsh Canal: already moored in the basin was the small cabin cruiser *Heron* owned by the Grundy family of Liverpool. With the help of their two sons, Christopher and Martin, Mr and Mrs Grundy had decided to venture up the Welsh Canal and see how far they could get. As we had precisely the same intention we agreed there and then to set off together so that we could render each other assistance as necessary.

We had both heard a rumour that the wooden drawbridge over the canal at Wrenbury had been damaged and could not be lifted. On the previous day, however, we had moored at Hack Green Locks on the main line whence it was but a short walk over to Wrenbury to inspect the bridge. We found, much to our surprise, that repairs had been completed the previous day, so we were able to reassure the Grundys that at least one obstacle had been removed.

Anticipating difficulty, I had equipped us with new spare cotton lines and a set of pulley blocks which were soon to prove their worth. At first everything went deceptively smoothly; we climbed successfully up the locks at Hurleston and Swanley and found the travelling between them much better than we had expected. It was at Lock No. 9, Baddiley, that the first serious hitch occurred when *Cressy* stuck fast half-way into the empty chamber.

It is a weakness of the orthodox design of a masonry lock chamber that its side walls are apt to be forced inwards owing to the action of frost in the surrounding ground. That the disused Welsh Canal locks had been affected in this way by two very severe winters in the past six years was a contingency that I had failed to take into account. A narrow boat slides into a narrow lock chamber with only inches to spare at the best of times, so it does not need much deformation to create an impasse such as now occurred. Despite the efforts of helpful lengthmen, using extra lines and the pulley blocks, or alternately lifting and dropping the top gate paddles to create a 'flush', *Cressy* refused to budge. Fortunately, however, the lower pound was a short one and the Baddiley lock keeper finally suggested lowering its level by drawing off water at the lock below. It was a risky expedient, for either *Cressy* might fail to drop with the water level or, if too much water was released, she could come to rest on the bottom sill. Happily neither of these disasters occurred and the device worked; *Cressy* suddenly dropped free and floated easily into the lock. But as the lock was filled, how anxiously we watched to ensure that she continued to rise with the water!

As our boat slowly rose above the upper gate, our hearts sank at the prospect before us. The canal ahead appeared to contain more weed than water, so much so that it looked solid enough to walk on. Even by frequent reversals to unwind the weed from the propeller, it was impossible to make progress at more than a snail's pace; while *Heron*, with her small propeller, was an even worse case. We ended up with *Heron* in tow behind *Cressy* while every available hand bow-hauled both from the towpath, our engine giving what assistance it could. Matters were made more difficult by the fact that the trouble at the lock had undoubtedly lowered the water level quite considerably. We therefore soon agreed to call it a day in the hope that overnight the water would rise somewhat and so make the going a little easier.

At this point I should explain why, during the whole of this first voyage up the Welsh Canal, we were dogged by a persistent shortage of water. The canal draws its water supply from the river Dee at the so-called 'Horseshoe Falls', actually a diversion weir built by Thomas Telford, the engineer of the canal, at Llantisilio. The original Ellesmere Canal Act which authorized construction contained a clause which stipulated that this water was to be used for navigational purposes only, and eventually returned to the river at Chester. In the 1940s, however, the Dee Conservators discovered that the canal owners, the L.M. & S. Railway, were selling canal water in considerable volume to the Monsanto Chemical Company whose works now occupy the site of William Hazeldine's Plas Kynaston Ironworks where the iron trough of the Pont Cysyllte aqueduct was cast. Somewhat naturally the conservators decided that if anybody sold water to this large chemical plant it should be themselves, and they forthwith successfully challenged the railway company in the courts. As a result of this legal action, the canal intake was limited to a stipulated quantity per day; and to ensure that this was not exceeded, the railway company were to install a flow meter at Llantisilio. At the time we made this first voyage, this flow meter and the house which contained it were still under construction, and in the meantime water was being admitted to the canal in extremely meagre quantities through a temporary by-pass channel. Yet even if this supply had been more generous, it is doubtful if it would have helped us very much, for the canal was so choked with weeds that the water would not flow down. Consequently it could be running over the spill weirs at the Llangollen end while at New Martin locks, twelve miles downstream, it could be nine inches low. The Welsh Canal supplies a reservoir at Hurleston which, in turn, supplies the main line of the Shropshire Union between Hack Green, Chester and Ellesmere Port. So it was not only the Welsh Canal which suffered from this parlous water situation.

We awoke next morning to find that the water level in the canal had risen slightly and we were able to struggle on as far as the repaired drawbridge at Wrenbury. Here there was a turning place or 'winding hole' where, despite its disused and depressing appearance, we reckoned we might be able to turn *Cressy*. I have never been one who throws in the sponge lightly, so it is a measure of the appalling state of the canal that we seriously considered making a strategic retreat to Hurleston. Before making a final decision, however, I lifted down Angela's bicycle from the deck and cycled along the towpath to see what conditions were like ahead. There appeared to be more water and less weed so we decided to forge on.

Soon bow-hauling was no longer necessary, but a rising cross wind made progress increasingly difficult for *Cressy*, and at teatime we decided to moor up for the night above Marbury Lock, leaving *Heron* to go ahead as the Grundys were anxious to ascend the lock flight at Grindley Brook before nightfall.

We eventually reached Grindley Brook only to find that

Cressy again stuck fast between the wing walls of the bottom lock. It was only after repeated 'flushing' from the top paddles that eventually, to our great relief, she came free and we were able to tie up to the bank below the lock. Here we held a council of war. Somehow or other we had to get *Cressy* up the Grindley Brook flight, for the prospect of retreat now did not bear thinking about; it would have meant stern-hauling our heavy boat back to that 'winding hole' at Wrenbury, and even there it was by no means certain that we could turn her. The day was Sunday, and we walked up to the lock house at the top of the flight where we explained our predicament to the lock keeper, Mr Howell, who promised to come down with an assistant to give us a hand next morning.

I spent most of the rest of the day planing obvious high spots off *Cressy*'s wooden hull. I also greased her bow rubbing strakes, for I had resolved upon the desperate expedient of driving her at full speed towards the lock chamber. If she went in, well and good; if she did not, I realized that nothing would free her short of partly demolishing a lock wall as Brunel and Claxton had had to do in order to get the *Great Britain* out of Bristol Docks. There was another snag to this scheme: to be quite certain that she was well and truly in the lock chamber, I would have to keep her going full ahead so long that it would be extremely difficult to prevent her cannoning violently into the top gate sill. Such a disaster could only be averted if Angela checked her at the right moment with a 'stern strap' and at the same instant all the top gate paddles were raised.

When Mr Howell and his mate appeared next morning I explained my plan to him and, though he looked extremely dubious, as well he might, he agreed that it was the only thing to do under the circumstances. So, having secured everything on board that might be damaged by a possible impact, we moved *Cressy* astern for fifty yards or so and then, with a silent prayer, I gave her full ahead and approached the narrow chamber at what appeared to be an impossible speed. Everything worked perfectly. There was a creaking sound and I felt her check slightly as the side walls nipped her, but the next moment she was through. Angela had checked her with the stern line, Mr Howell had raised the top paddles, and a few seconds later the

109

lower gates had slammed to behind me with a crash. I felt
Cressy surge upwards. So far so good, but there were still five
more locks to go, culminating in a triple lock staircase of awe-
some depth. It was so many years since a narrow boat had
passed through the canal that Mr Howell was as much in the
dark as we were as to the likely outcome of our venture. In the
event, *Cressy* stuck again firmly coming out of the third lock and
I had to use our pulley blocks to free her; yet, curiously enough,
although the lock keeper had dire misgivings about the state of
the staircase, she came through it without the slightest difficulty.
It was with immense relief that we moored opposite Mr
Howell's cottage at the top of the flight and caught a bus into
Whitchurch to do our weekly shopping.

One could see from the weir beside the top lock that the canal
level was at least six inches below normal; and in order to
keep the lower part of the canal and Hurleston reservoir
supplied, Mr Howell had the special by-pass paddle drawn. A
very long level now lay ahead of us, so we could not expect any
improvement but must make the best of it. As soon as we
started off, it was obvious that the bottom was much too near
the top. Happily, however, there was little or no weed and we
were able to make slow but steady progress under our own
power for a mile or two until we reached a point which, according to that canal traveller's bible, de Salis's *Guide*, was known
as Blackoe Cottages. Here *Cressy* ran suddenly and firmly
aground in mid-channel; so firmly, in fact, that her bows rose
up out of the water. Investigation soon showed that a small
stream flowed into the canal at this point and that over the
years it had built up a bar of silt that extended from bank to
bank.

Once again my pulley blocks and extra lines proved invalu-
able. Just above the mouth of the brook grew a stout tree whose
bole made an ideal anchor for my double block, the single
block being hooked on to *Cressy's* fore-end stud. Then the free
end of the cotton line was taken across the canal to the towpath
where a long pull and a strong pull by Angela and myself,
assisted by most of the astonished inhabitants of Blackoe
Cottages, was sufficient to drive *Cressy* through the silt barrier.
We then had lunch before continuing slowly on our way as far

as the old wharf and bridge at Platt Lane where we found a party of gypsies encamped in a green road and stopped for a cup of tea to satisfy a mutual curiosity.

As recounted in the first volume of this autobiography, it was over this same Welsh canal that I had made my first voyage by inland waterway in 1930 at a time when *Cressy* was steam driven. The canal had seemed to me then to be so uniquely and magically beautiful that I was at once captivated by the idea of travelling by waterway. This narrow and winding ribbon of water conveyed such a strange sense of remoteness and seemed to pass through such an astonishing variety of scenery. Now, returning to the same canal in the same boat after the lapse of seventeen years I was interested to discover whether my first impressions had been correct, or whether I had been beguiled by distance and nostalgia. I could still recall vividly the enchantment of that first voyage, gliding through the glassy waters on that spring morning so long ago. I recalled ruefully that it had then been easy going and not a perpetual struggle with weed, lack of water and decaying lock chambers. Yet despite all the effort and anxiety, I decided as we left Platt Lane that it was worth it; the magic remained; it was no illusion.

At Platt Lane the Welsh Canal undergoes its first dramatic transformation. Up to this point we had been travelling through a typical Cheshire countryside of gently rolling pastures and large dairy farms of blackish red brick; a pleasant enough scene but somewhat tame. Now we suddenly found ourselves in a landscape that reminded us of our last year's journey across the great Bog of Allen on the Grand Canal of Ireland. Whixall Moss is indeed a replica of an Irish turf bog set down on the Shropshire/Cheshire borders, and the Welsh Canal cuts straight across it. For some reason, presumably connected with the nature of the peat, the canal becomes not only weed-free but both wider and deeper as soon as it enters upon the bog, so that from crawling along at snail's pace *Cressy* was suddenly able to travel as fast as upon some broad river. They had been cutting turf on the Moss, and the dark stacks of drying peats in the middle distance backed by the distant shapes of the Berwyns beyond, serenely blue and indistinct in the haze of the summer's day, made the resemblance to an Irish landscape complete.

We reached the end of Whixall Moss all too soon and once again the canal became narrow, shallow and winding, its banks lined with the yellow flowers of musk. But we were now in the wilder border country, quite unlike the broad pastures of Cheshire. Presently we reached the little village of Bettisfield where we decided to moor for the night. Politically, *Cressy* had now entered Wales for the first time since 1930, for Bettisfield is in 'Flintshire detached', that strange little Welsh island in Shropshire. Physically, however, those distant blue mountains marked the true Welsh border whither we were bound – or so I hoped.

After dinner that evening we strolled down the road into the village and had a drink at the 'Nag's Head'. The first thing I noticed as we entered the small tap room was a broken luggage rack bracket out of a railway coach reposing in a glass case on the wall. I had encountered some queer objects in pubs in my time, but nothing as odd as this. On inquiry, it transpired that this was a relic of the Welshampton railway disaster which took place on the main line of the old Cambrian Railway that runs parallel with the canal at this point. Apart from the better known – and worse – accident at Abermule, Welshampton was the only serious disaster that the Cambrian suffered.

A little distance beyond Bettisfield, the Welsh Canal springs a second surprise, comparable in beauty to Whixall Moss though of an entirely different character. It passes through the heart of what is sometimes called the Shropshire Lake District, a number of shallow, tree-fringed meres in the neighbourhood of the little town of Ellesmere. The water of these meres normally appears dark and peaty, especially under the shade of the encircling trees, but once a year a brief phenomenon, known locally as the 'break', occurs when a species of algae rises to the surface to turn the water an opaque green. Ellesmere itself, the largest of these meres, is also the most open and the most frequented, being the nearest to the town. By contrast, Colemere (pronounced 'Coomer' by the locals) and Blake Mere are tree-surrounded and secluded, the haunt of many wild-fowl. The canal passes close beside them and I remembered the impression they had made upon me when I had first seen them from *Cressy*'s deck in the grey stillness of an early spring dawn.

Now under the clear light of the summer sun I found they had lost nothing of their earlier enchantment. We moored up under the shade of the trees beside the narrow bank that divides the canal from Colemere and had a very protracted picnic lunch, interrupted only by the intermittent clucking and splashing of the coot and moorhen which alone flawed the mirror of the water. We felt it was a fitting reward for all the effort and anxieties involved in forcing a passage through waters which, in the course of recent years, had become virtually uncharted. Yet how many times, I reflected, must *Cressy* have passed this way in the course of her working life when she was one of the Shropshire Union Canal Carrying Company's fleet or, later, when she belonged to the owners of a mill at Maesbury.

Although the going had been slow since we left Whixall Moss, the canal had been pleasantly free from weed; but after lunch, as we passed through the very short Ellesmere tunnel, we saw that the canal ahead was choked with a dense blanket of green. So thick was it that it was only with the help of bow-hauling from the towpath that we covered the brief remaining distance to the junction of the short Ellesmere branch canal. At this point, the main line of canal curves sharply southward, rounding Beech House, once the headquarters of the old Ellesmere Canal Company, and the extensive canal workshops.* As at Wrenbury, we decided once again that discretion was the better part of valour and that it would be better to explore what lay ahead on foot before passing so convenient a turning point for *Cressy*. What we saw ahead could scarcely have been more discouraging; the canal was choked with dense weed as far as the eye could see. Moreover, we were told at the canal workshops that this state of things prevailed at least as far as New Marton locks and that even if we fought our way through this Sargasso Sea of weed, we could go no further than Chirk because a slip in the deep cutting to the north of Chirk tunnel had made the canal quite impassable.

So, once again, despite all our efforts, my ambition to take *Cressy* over Pont Cysyllte had been defeated; the way into Wales was closed to us, and it then seemed most unlikely that

* Although situated on a disused canal, in 1947 these workshops were still very active, making lock-gates for the whole of the Shropshire Union Canal system.

it would ever reopen. Sadly, we swung *Cressy* about in the mouth of the junction and tied her up alongside the towpath by Beech House. Although this was convenient for the town it was by no means ideal in other respects; so, as we had planned to stay in the area for several summer weeks, we determined to retrace our steps for three and a half miles to a disused wharf at Hampton Bank which had looked both inviting and convenient when we had passed it by.

Hampton Bank Wharf did indeed prove to be an almost ideal mooring. It lay just off the road from Ellesmere to Wem which then carried little traffic and from which the wharf was readily accessible. Although the wharf was grass-grown it provided a good hard standing for a car. A solitary cottage – obviously built for a wharfinger – was still occupied by a kindly country couple who gladly supplied us with drinking water and kept an eye on the boat when we were away. Here I left Angela in charge of *Cressy* while I travelled by train to Banbury for the purpose of collecting my Alvis.

During these summer weeks at Hampton Bank, despite having the Alvis, we made good use of the local railway system – in this case part of what had once been the old Cambrian Railway – for the sheer pleasure of sampling rural branch lines. It was a hobby which combined well with living afloat. We used that part of the Cambrian main line which keeps the canal company most of the way between Whitchurch, Ellesmere and Oswestry. We also travelled to Wrexham by the branch line from Ellesmere and, best of all, trundled up the Tanat Valley branch from Oswestry to Llanrhaiadr y Mochnant in a diminutive train of Cambrian four-wheelers, now smartly painted in G.W.R. livery; it was drawn by a little tank engine, the *Lady Margaret*, which had originally seen service on the Liskeard & Looe Railway in faraway Cornwall but had now come north to work out her last days in this remote Welsh valley.

From mid-July to mid-August, while *Cressy* lay at Hampton Bank, the weather was exceptionally fine and warm. Pleasant though it was, this four-week spell of heat and unbroken drought began to affect the canal. At first it was only a matter of an inch or two, but then the level suddenly began to fall alarmingly. Inquiries elicited the gloomy information that there had been a burst in the canal bank in the neighbourhood of Chirk and that in consequence the temporary feed from the Dee at Llantisilio had been shut off pending repairs. We had entered this abandoned canal at our own risk and peril and had no rights whatever; *Cressy* could sit on the mud at Hampton Bank until doomsday for all the L.M.S. railway cared, so it was up to us to do something quickly. For a while, business was brisk in the telephone kiosk at Hampton Bank. It was obvious that so long as Mr Howell, the lock keeper at Grindley Brook, continued to draw water down through his by-pass culvert into the canal below the locks, the situation would worsen rapidly. On the telephone he sounded most anxious to help, but said he dared not shut off supplies to Hurleston reservoir without authority from Crewe. So, in response to an S.O.S. message to Crewe, a remote official in the L.M.S. finally agreed somewhat grudgingly that Howell could drop his by-pass paddle for twenty-four hours and no longer. All this took place on a Sunday (17 August), and by the time we had got confirmation from Howell that he had complied with instructions it was 6 p.m. We got under way without more ado, travelling in close company with *Heron*. We were dragging the bottom as far as Bettisfield, but after this the going improved somewhat and by 9 p.m. we had reached Platt Lane Wharf, where we decided to lie for the night.

Remembering our experience on the upward journey, it was obvious that the toughest part of this race against the clock was still to come, but fortunately help was at hand in the person of one of the early members of the I.W.A. and his wife. He was a sterling character named Livock, an ex-R.A.F. Squadron Leader who, before the war, had pioneered the flying-boat route to Singapore. Precisely how we got in touch with each other at this providential moment I cannot now remember and my log is silent on the subject. Suffice it to say that Livock and his wife drove on to Platt Lane Wharf in a large estate car promptly at 9 a.m. the next morning. We then proceeded to discharge from *Cressy's* aft hold everything that could be spared – five gallon drums of spare fuel, off-cuts of locomotive frame-plates from Kerr Stuart which had been serving as ballast ever since those far-off days at Stoke-on-Trent when *Cressy* had been steam-driven. All this was loaded into the back of the estate car. It settled down on its back springs rather like a broody hen, but at the same time *Cressy*'s stern rose out of the water nearly two inches. At a time when every inch counted, this was probably crucial. The transfer completed, Mrs Livock then set off in the car with instructions to keep in touch so far as possible until – we hoped – we were able to switch cargoes again at Basin End, Nantwich. Her husband remained with us to supply the extra muscle power which we would certainly need. *Cressy* then set off, towing *Heron* astern and with Angela, Livock and Christopher Grundy bow-hauling from the towpath. Their efforts were only occasionally needed until we reached Blackoe Cottages where, remembering the trouble we had previously had with the shoal across the canal, I thought we would most probably meet our Waterloo. Once more I rigged our blocks and tackle, but this time it was a much tougher proposition. For a long time, strain as we would, *Cressy* refused to budge until finally a team of nine, the combined crews of both boats, plus Livock, plus three able-bodied recruits from the Cottages, were mustered together on the towpath. Digging in our heels and heaving like a tug-o'-war team, we suddenly felt the line give in our hands and, with mutual cries of encouragement, we fought our way backward foot by foot as we watched *Cressy* drive partly through and partly over the obstruction. It was an immense relief to see her floating once more and on the 'home' side of the barrier. We celebrated victory by calling a brief halt for a lunch that consisted mainly of very welcome liquor.

Lack of water had worsened the weed problem, and when we continued after lunch we several times had to resort to bow-hauling for this reason. But now that our main concern was to stay afloat, weeds seemed a relatively minor worry. So, partly under power and partly bow-hauled, our boats arrived at Grindley Brook, with a very tired and sweaty crew in attendance, at 4 p.m. or just two hours inside our twenty-four-hour time limit. Mr Howell was delighted to see us. He had expected to see *Heron* but confessed that he had had grave doubts whether *Cressy* would be able to make it. Now, with her bows nudging the top gate of the triple staircase lock while we brewed a cup of tea, I no longer had any fear that we might be stranded. Once on the other side of that gate, there was no doubt at all in my mind that Mr Howell would let down enough water to float us back to Hurleston even if it meant emptying the entire upper portion of the canal. And so it proved. Looking down, we could see that the short pound between the bottom of the staircase and Lock No. 16 was completely dry, and both our boats had to lie in the chambers of the staircase while water was passed down to fill it. The bottom lock at Grindley Brook, where we had stuck so fast on the upward journey, did not delay us this time. With all the top paddles up and her engine going full ahead, *Cressy* shot out of that lock chamber like a cork from a champagne bottle. But not far, for the canal below the flight looked so low that we decided to tie up for the night to allow the pound to make up. After all, we were no longer working to a deadline and time was now on our side.

Our progress next day was very slow but sure, for now we were literally bringing with us the precious water we needed. This meant that there had to be lengthy pauses at each lock while we ran the water down from the pound above to the pound below. Apart from this there is little to say about the last stage of our adventurous foray up the Welsh Section. We spent the next night at the head of Baddiley top lock, and at 6 p.m. on the evening of the day following we moored in Nantwich Basin where we were able to relieve Mrs Livock of her car load of fuel and ballast. We celebrated victory that night with a protracted and memorable dinner at the 'Crown Hotel' in Nantwich. Everyone was in high good humour, for there is nothing to equal the power of an episode of this kind as a generator of friendship and fellow-feeling.

Next day we parted company, *Heron* sailing north towards Chester, while *Cressy* swung her bows southward. Our destination was Gayton Arm End, where the Northampton Branch of the Grand Union Canal joins the main line of that canal near Blisworth. We travelled via the Staffordshire & Worcestershire and the Trent & Mersey canals, and the rivers Trent and Soar to Leicester, where we joined the Leicester Section of the Grand Union. This whole journey of 203 miles from Hampton Bank Wharf on the Welsh Marches to Northamptonshire took sixteen days and I recorded the fact that throughout this time we enjoyed unbroken sunshine.

There was a particular reason why we had made Gayton and not Banbury our immediate objective. During our stay at Hampton Bank I had been pondering over possible ways of attracting new members to our Association and publicizing its canal crusade, and had hit on the notion of staging a canal exhibition in London. The great question was *where*, for the infant I.W.A. certainly could not afford to hire any gallery in central London. Then I thought of Anthony Heal whom I had known since the earliest days of the Vintage Sports Car Club at the Phoenix. Anthony received my idea enthusiastically, and readily agreed that we might use the Mansard Gallery outside the restaurant on the top floor of the Heal family's famous shop in Tottenham Court Road. With this satisfactorily settled it became a question of collecting suitable material for exhibition, and we had agreed that Gayton was the most convenient base from which to pursue this quest. Not only was it conveniently near the main line to Euston, but the Grand Union carried a much larger floating population than did the Oxford Canal. There was a third reason also. At Gayton Junction were situated the canal workshops for the district, and the home and offices of the district engineer, C. N. Hadlow. Charles Hadlow was a friend of mine and a canal engineer of wide experience with a deep interest in the canal past. So much so that, on his retirement, he played a great part in the setting up of the present Waterways Museum at Stoke Bruerne of which he became honorary curator. I guessed – rightly as things turned out – that he would be the best person to assist us in locating suitable material for display. It so happened that he had lately discovered, in an old loft over one of the canal buildings at Gayton, a pile of old glass-plate negatives, all showing early canal scenes, which had been taken by his predecessors. To examine this treasure-trove in his office, holding them up to the light and deciding which ones to print up, was a fascinating exercise. Charles Hadlow was able to lend us a pair of the brass armlets which were issued by the old Grand Junction Canal Company to the professional 'leggers' who had once been responsible for propelling the boats through Blisworth tunnel at 1*s*. 6*d*. a time. This was only one of the many two- and three-dimensional objects – boat furniture, traditional boaters' clothing, model boats, some made by professionals and others by the boatmen themselves – which we managed to collect in a surprisingly short space of time, for we had arrived at Gayton on 4 September and the Exhibition was due to open on 25 October. The find which most pleased me was a splendid diorama showing a pair of horse-drawn narrow boats entering the top lock at Stoke Bruerne. I cannot remember how we got to know of the existence of this, but I remember collecting it from its owner's garage in the suburbs of Leighton Buzzard. He explained that, with other dioramas, it had been made by his father many years before.

Angela and I spent several days arranging all this material in Heals' Mansard Gallery, an unfamiliar and satisfying task which we thoroughly enjoyed and which we were able to complete on time despite frequent interruptions. We walked in fear of one formidable lady of middle age who was in charge of the gallery and very evidently disapproved of our amateurish goings-on. She seemed to lurk perpetually in a little office in a corner of the gallery from which she would dart out at us from time to time whenever she observed us in the act of committing some dire offence such as sticking drawing pins into the woodwork. Altogether more encouraging and enjoyable were the visits of Anthony's father, old Sir Ambrose Heal, who took a lively and intelligent interest in our enterprise.

This 'Inland Waterways Exhibition' proved a great success. It attracted so much attention from press and public that I succeeded in persuading some commercial firm (I forget the name) to pack up the exhibition when it closed at Heals after a month and take it on a tour of provincial art galleries at no cost to the Association. One tragi-comic result of this was that the firm's packers, who were experts at this class of work, discovered that our precious Stoke Bruerne diorama was riddled with woodworm. The discovery that someone was suffering from bubonic plague could scarcely have created a greater furore. The unfortunate model was at once isolated and subjected to such a barrage of poisonous sprays that it finally disintegrated and was never heard of again so far as I can remember. Its owner took its loss philosophically since it was obvious that it had become infested during its long years of neglect in his garage. At least his father's patient craftsmanship had enjoyed one final blaze of glory.

Chapter 6

Sharpness and the Northern Canals

With our work on the Exhibition completed, there was no longer any reason for remaining at Gayton, so we headed for our familiar winter base at Tooley's Yard, Banbury, arriving there on 14 November. Here we lay until 10 April of the following year (1948) when we once again headed north and west towards the Severn. This time, however, we proposed to turn south at Worcester and to go downstream as far as Sharpness. Also, as a variation, we decided not to take the Stratford Canal at Kingswood but to carry straight on up the Grand Union Canal to Birmingham, and so via Digbeth and the Farmer's Bridge locks to a junction with the Worcester & Birmingham Canal at Worcester Bar. It was a leisurely journey. We first of all spent three weeks at Braunston boatyard, having obtained permission from our friend Frank Nurser to repaint our cabin sides in the shelter of the covered dock there,* before returning to Napton Junction to pick up the route to Birmingham. Then followed a fortnight at Tardebigge and three weeks in Diglis Basin at Worcester, so it was high summer before we finally set off down the river, spending the next night at Tewkesbury, turning aside on to the Avon and lying along the bank of the Mythe meadow opposite Healing's mill.

I shall never forget that mooring in Tewkesbury. It was a perfect summer's evening, cloudless and still after a warm day; no noise of traffic reached us and ancient Tewkesbury seemed the quintessence of a quiet and peaceful country town. It

* In this covered dock, the steam narrow boats of Messrs Fellows, Morton & Clayton had once transhipped their cargoes.

radiated a tranquillity that was soon to be lost and never to be
known again. On the Mythe meadow, corncrakes called to each
other repeatedly as the sun went down behind the Malverns
and a thick mist began to rise over the wide expanse of grass.
The harsh call of this strangely elusive bird, sounding now here,
now there, reminds me of the whirring of grasshoppers vastly
amplified. It always brings back my childhood, for I often heard
it in the small, summer hayfields of the Welsh Border; but
now mechanical reapers have almost banished it and, although
I have heard the corncrake since in Ireland, this was its last
performance in England so far as I am concerned.

There was thick mist over the Mythe next morning presaging
another glorious day. The sun was warm on our backs and our
decks hot to the touch by the time we passed through Tewkesbury Lock and set off down the river towards Gloucester at a
fine pace, passing fishermen, out in their black Severn punts,
netting for salmon in the reach between Deerhurst and Apperley.
At all seasons of the year, Severn flows faster than Thames
because it is much less heavily locked. In this $28\frac{1}{2}$ miles of river,
from the tail of Diglis Locks at Worcester to the entrance to
Gloucester Docks, there is but the one solitary lock at Upper
Lode, Tewkesbury. Compared with the translucent reaches of
the Thames, still as a lake except in times of heavy flood,
Severn is a powerful river, a great body of dark water eternally
flowing swiftly and silently down to the sea. We speak of
'Father Thames' and think of him as a jolly old soul, whereas
Severn is feminine. Those who know this river speak of Severn,
never 'the Severn', and usually refer to the river as 'she'.
Sabrina may be fair, but if she is indeed feminine then hers is
a sombre and subtle Celtic beauty, menacing and not to be
slighted. Yet for the men who know her most intimately, as
did Harry Rogers of Ironbridge, she holds a fascination that is
almost hypnotic. Although my first-hand knowledge of Severn
was brief, it was long enough for me to realize that she was not
to be trifled with – especially when one is piloting a large and
under-powered boat. The Model T Ford might be an ideal
engine for propelling a 70-foot narrow boat in the still waters
of the canals, but it was immediately obvious that on Severn it
was woefully inadequate. Astern it was generally impossible

to hold *Cressy* against the current, while travelling upstream between Gloucester and Worcester was, as we were later to find, a painfully slow and tedious business.

For craft travelling downstream as we were, the approach to Gloucester is particularly tricky, for above the city, at Upper Parting, the river splits into two streams; on the right is the old Maisemore Channel with its single lock. This is the old line of navigation. It communicates with the tidal river and was used before the Gloucester & Berkeley Ship Canal was opened in 1827. It was still used for many years after this by masters of Severn trows who preferred the hazards and uncertainties of the estuary rather than pay the toll charges on the canal. This old channel is now quite disused and all downstream traffic takes the left-hand channel that leads to Gloucester Lock and so into Gloucester Docks. This is half the width of the river above, the current runs swiftly and it is extremely tortuous. In 1948 we faced an additional hazard in the shape of the large petrol tanker barges trading between Avonmouth and oil depots at Worcester and Stourport. This traffic was then considerable and the tankers as large as Severn could handle. A laden tanker could only just round these tight turns on the Gloucester channel and needed all its width to do so. Therefore, owing to our inability to stop, to have encountered one in such a situation would have meant an almost certain collision. As we remembered, the narrow boat *Heather Bell*, which I mentioned earlier in this book, was coming up the Gloucester & Berkeley Canal one morning in thick fog with a cargo of grain from Sharpness when she was in collision with an empty tanker whose high bows suddenly loomed out of the fog ahead. She sank instantly. Fortunately, for craft heading downstream as we were, it was possible to predict fairly accurately when and where laden tanker barges would be encountered because they could only enter Sharpness Docks from the river at high water, and their running time up the canal to Gloucester was remarkably consistent. We had therefore armed ourselves with a local tide table and so were able to enter the Gloucester channel at a time when the risk of our encountering another large craft was minimal.

If, as was the case with us, Gloucester Lock is not set for

downstream craft, the entry to Gloucester Docks is decidedly
tricky because the river channel sweeps past the tail of the lock
and then almost directly over Gloucester weir en route for the
Lower Parting. Moreover, there is no towing path hereabouts,
only a high quay wall on our left. A signal indicated to us the
state of the lock, but by the time we sighted this we had to act
quickly. Fortunately, in our haste we did not forget the lesson
we had learned on the Thames eight years before – to hold her
by the stern. Angela jumped nimbly from the bow to the quay
stairs and I then threw her up a stern line. After that it was all
plain sailing; we found a quiet berth beside an old brick ware-
house in the docks where we lay until the next morning.

The Gloucester & Berkeley Canal does not go to Berkeley
although it has borne that name ever since it was first conceived
in 1793. With its swift currents, its shifting sand bars and its
tremendous tides (spring tides can rise thirty-four feet), not to
mention its famous bore, the Severn estuary is as dangerous a
piece of water as any in the world, and it was the purpose of
the canal to by-pass its upper portion from Berkeley Pill to
Gloucester. It was conceived from the first as a ship canal,
seventy feet wide and fifteen feet deep. These were ambitious
figures in eighteenth-century England; indeed they were over-
ambitious, for the project soon ran into such dire physical and
financial difficulties that it was not completed until April 1827.
By that time the original engineer, Robert Mylne, and several
successors, had come and gone and it was Thomas Telford who
finally completed it. In 1818, it was decided to increase the
depth of the canal to eighteen feet but to make Sharpness Point
the site of the junction with the river, so reducing its length by
one and a half miles.

To travel from Gloucester to Sharpness was a novel experience, for *Cressy* had never known a canal of this character before.
There are no locks but many swing bridges, manned by
bridge-keepers who, we found, lived in delightful little cottages
which, with their classical, pillared porticos, would not have
looked out of place as lodges on some great estate. At the
Gloucester end of the canal these swing bridges were sufficiently high to allow *Cressy* to pass beneath them without
disturbing their keepers, but after this they became lower so

that we had to alert their attendants by sounding the regulation two blasts on our air horn. With such a wide, deep and lock-free channel, with bridges opening before us at our bidding, there was nothing whatever for me to do except to lean upon the tiller. As soon as the sun had dissolved the morning haze it became very hot and I am ashamed to say that I must have fallen into a kind of daze or day-dream, lulled by the steady throb of the engine. From this I was rudely disturbed by the loud blast of a ship's siren behind me. It was as though someone had suddenly sounded a loud raspberry on a trombone just behind my ear. I nearly jumped out of my skin and looked round to see the grey bows of a steamer looming up just astern. It was only the very small coaster *Monkton Combe* of Bristol which we had earlier seen unloading at Gloucester; but, being empty, her bows rose high out of the water so that from my lowly vantage it looked as if we were about to be run down by the *Queen Mary*. Needless to say I lost no time in drawing into the side and slowing down to let this monster past. This was a manoeuvre that gave me some anxious moments for, in so narrow a channel, even with light draught and her engine going slow ahead, the *Monkton Combe*'s passing exercised considerable 'draw' on us so that it was not easy to avoid a side-long collision. Hardly had the ship vanished round a bend ahead than there appeared coming towards us the steam tug *Speedwell* with a train of barges in tow. In contrast to the deep-noted drumming of the *Monkton Combe*'s diesel, the *Speedwell* slid past us in silent dignity; the metronomic rhythm of her compound engine running slow ahead was only just audible, and a wisp of black smoke curled lazily from her funnel. Travelling by ship canal was more eventful than we had thought.

As we had all the time in the world and these were new waters to us, we decided to stay for two nights at Saul Junction, almost exactly half-way between Gloucester and Sharpness. Here the ship canal cuts across the old Stroudwater canal which, until the Thames & Severn canal became impassable, was a link in the through route between the two rivers. Now the Stroudwater had also become derelict and we moored on the only fragment of it that was still navigable – a length of three hundred yards east of the junction which was used as a leat, feeding water into the ship canal from the river Frome. The two miles of the Stroudwater between the junction and the estuary has been derelict for a very long time, for little traffic can have passed that way since the ship canal was opened.* After we had had tea, we walked the towpath of this long disused section of canal, past the 'Junction Inn', until we came to the old tidal entrance lock at Framilode and looked out across the estuary, watching the strong tide making and submerging the sand flats with astonishing speed.

Although I would not care to live in such a place myself, there is a strange fascination about the flat lands bordering the estuary of a great river, particularly when, as in this case, navigation is hazardous and the channel is too wide to be easily bridged. Such a natural barrier creates on its banks unfrequented hinterlands where roads lead nowhere or peter out in the rotting timber stagings of forgotten ferries, forlorn amid mud-banks where waders walk delicately. The main roads from Gloucester to Bristol and South Wales seem to draw the boundaries of modern urban civilization, and in the littoral between them lies an empty quarter where old trades and old ways still persist – or they did in 1948. For example, at Saul there was a dry dock that looked as though it pre-dated the ship canal and on its stocks lay the Severn trow *Water Witch* undergoing repairs; she had long since lost her mast and was working as a dumb barge carrying Dean coal between Lydney harbour and Bristol, but there was no mistaking her lineage.

We spent twenty-four hours exploring the Saul neighbourhood before setting off to cover the last eight miles of our voyage to Sharpness. The most dramatic moment of that voyage came just after we had passed through the little village of Purton. Hereabouts the ship canal makes a sweeping S-bend and then, for the last mile and a quarter, runs parallel with the shore line of the estuary with only a sea wall separating the two. The tide was out and from our deck we looked out over a great expanse of sand to the foothills of Dean Forest rising from the further shore. Ahead, the many lattice-girder spans of the Severn railway bridge emphasized the breadth of the

* There was possibly a little traffic in Dean coal from Bullo Pill on the opposite side of Severn to Stroud and wharves on the Thames & Severn.

estuary. The bridge was silhouetted against the westering sunlight and beyond it rose Sharpness Point and the docks.

The junction of the ship canal with the estuary was originally made on the upstream side of the red sandstone cliff of the Point, so that the entrance lock and the berths above it were sheltered to some extent from the force of the incoming tides and from the prevailing south-westerlies. In November, 1874, however, the New Docks were opened on the inland side of the point with a new and much larger entrance lock further downstream. This development was a result of the increase in the tonnage of shipping. If ships were too big to travel up the canal to Gloucester, at least they might be lured upriver away from Avonmouth either to discharge their cargoes or tranship them into barges or narrow boats in the new docks. The effect of this change was that Sharpness Point became an island, accessible only by swing bridges, and that the old entrance fell derelict.

Because I have always been fascinated by docks, I had paid several visits to Sharpness Docks long ago when I was working as an engineering apprentice at Dursley. It made a sad spectacle in those days of the great slump. The new docks had become a berth for rusting, idle shipping, while the old entrance lock and channel were derelict and choked with weeds. So, although I was familiar with the dock layout, returning after so many years I did not know what to expect but hoped it might be possible to moor in the old channel so as to be out of the way of traffic. Great was my surprise when we reached the junction to see a perfectly clear channel stretching away to my right and terminating in a very smart and obviously completely restored entrance lock. As I soon discovered, this work had been carried out as a war-time precaution in case the new entrance lock was damaged by enemy bombs. As soon as we made this pleasant discovery we put *Cressy* about at the junction, and came stern first into the old canal to find a perfect mooring alongside the disused towpath and the sea wall.

Here we lay for a memorable month of summer, from mid-June to mid-July and here, as was customary, I brought my 12/50 Alvis to serve as land transport. I had to park her on Sharpness Point near the top of a disused coal-drop immediately opposite our moorings, for to reach *Cressy* it was necessary to cross the old canal by the lock-gates. But this inconvenience was a small price to pay for our seclusion and for our splendid view over the estuary. One can never get to know a place or learn to savour its particularity without living in it. It was in this that our way of life proved so triumphantly successful. As now at Sharpness, *Cressy* would slide unobtrusively into some quiet mooring and at once we would feel at home and under the skin of the place. It was a pleasure which never palled. The fact that it is unknown to those who park caravans is something to do with the particular quality of boats and water. A boat is of necessity in her natural element whereas a caravan in a field is an intruder.

We certainly fell under Severn's spell during our stay at Sharpness. When we lay a-bed and heard the sound of the night tide rushing up the river or, on awakening, the crying of gulls and the piping of waders from beyond the sea-wall, it was easy to imagine we had put to sea. Between *Cressy's* stern and the lock there loomed the bows of the merchant navy training ship *Invicatrix*. Sometimes, when we were breakfasting, we would hear the rhythmical creak of rowlocks and look out to see a party of cadets at rowing practice in a ship's lifeboat. Neither they nor anyone else dared interfere with our boat while we were away, for we had the most zealous of watch-dogs in the person of old Mr Smith down at the lock-house.

Mr Smith was a retired Bristol Channel Pilot who was appointed lock keeper when the old canal entrance was restored. Happily his job was a sinecure because the Luftwaffe never visited Sharpness. A man who had spent a long lifetime in sailing ships could not have found a more appropriate shore berth. His lock-house stood on a breakwater that projected beyond the tip of the Point to protect the mouth of the lock from the force of the ebb tide. The windows of his living-room looked right and left up and down the estuary. When we were greatly privileged to be invited to supper there, I thought it one of the most remarkable rooms I had ever been in. It was like being on the bridge of a ship and hard to believe that we were not afloat – indeed the water running so swiftly past the windows created in the house an illusion of movement. But the old man would move no more. On the shore beneath the red cliff of the point lay the bare ribs of his Pilot Cutter, looking like the rib-cage of some huge stranded sea monster. Had she been mine I do not think I could have endured such a sight, but her captain was more philosophical. He was the most authentic old salt I have ever encountered. He would potter along to *Cressy* of an evening and, sitting at his ease in our cabin, tell us tales, wondrous tales, of manning the yards to shorten sail with the reeling ship tearing through the water as 'she ran her easting down' – a lovely phrase. He had harrowing stories of hard tack, of maggoty pork and weevily biscuits, of a ship becalmed and food running low: '. . . and when we opened that last barrel of flour it was half-full of rats' turds'. We listened spell-bound; if he had claimed to have shot the albatross I think we would have believed him.

When he finally left the mercantile marine and joined the Bristol Channel Pilots, life was only slightly less hard for the service was then highly competitive. To seek and claim a Channel-bound ship, the pilots in their sailing cutters would range far out to sea like so many predatory pirates. According to this old man, it was no uncommon thing to sail as far as the Bay of Biscay before they found a ship to bring in. This meant that to do his job and pay his way the pilot needed a sailing craft that would carry him fast and far and in every sort of weather; through some of the most dangerous waters in the world, with their huge tides, their short, steep seas and their prevailing on-shore winds. The result was the Bristol Channel Pilot Cutter. Although it has a hull so beamy that it looks like a tub, it is surprisingly fast and has been described as probably the finest sea-keeping boat ever evolved for British waters.

There seemed always to be something to see at Sharpness. Distant trains moving swiftly under plumes of steam along the far shore-line of the estuary as they headed for South Wales, or crawling slowly (for there was a severe speed restriction) and with rhythmical rumbling, across the Severn Bridge. Except for a unique push-and-pull train consisting of compartment stock which shuttled between Berkeley Road, Sharpness and Lydney, there was little traffic over the bridge except on Sundays when the Severn tunnel was closed and freight traffic diverted over the bridge. These Sundays-only goods trains were hauled by the ubiquitous G.W.R. 2–6–0 Moguls, as these were the heaviest locomotives allowed over the bridge. Then there was the traffic on the ship canal to watch. The barge traffic – mostly diesel-powered tankers – soon ceased to attract our attention, but in the case of the coastal shipping that occasionally traded to Gloucester it was quite otherwise, and we were always given an audible warning when such a ship was approaching. There are three swing bridges of varying height at Sharpness, two road bridges over the inland entrance to the new docks, and the railway bridge which, by a handsome margin, was the highest. It was the practice for captains to sound one, two or three toots on their sirens depending on how many bridges needed to be raised, so that three blasts was our signal that something big was coming down the canal – although once it proved to be only a small yacht with an exceptionally tall mast. The best thing about a ship canal is that it provides the unique experience of seeing a large sea-going ship gliding slowly and serenely along through green fields, a spectacle which always strikes me as bizarre as that of a locomotive puffing along a country road or a flying motor car.

Often we would walk down to the new entrance lock to watch traffic coming into the lock from the Channel and to admire the tremendous expertise displayed in this operation. Anyone who doubts the power of Severn's tide should stand, as we did, on the wooden jetty that projects beyond the wing-walls of Sharpness lock when the tide is making. There is such an immensely powerful and irresistible onrush of tidal current beneath one's feet, making the whole stout timber jetty tremble with its violence, that the wonder is that the Severn Bore does not become a tidal wave as all-powerful and terrifying as Lear's cataracts, drowning the cocks on all the steeples of the Severn Vale. Traffic bound upriver comes up on the tide from Avonmouth, and a signal at Sharpness, hoisted shortly before high water, indicates that craft may enter. The ideal aimed for, of course, is to arrive off Sharpness as soon as this signal is hoisted and so proceed straight into the lock, but conditions of wind, tide and traffic are so variable that this is seldom achieved even by the wiliest old hands. Boats either arrive too early or too late, in which case the lock is already fully occupied. In both cases they have to wait in the tidal channel, and with a tide running at anything up to six knots this means coming about and heading into it and then coming about once more when the time comes to enter the lock. Standing on the end of the jetty, we saw this manoeuvre performed many times and could appreciate how tricky and hazardous it was. We could understand how, on a foggy night in the autumn of 1939, a towing hawser had parted and several dumb barges were swept up the river with tragic loss of life.

Through the good offices of my friend Billy Bevington of Banbury, I had become something of a 'collector' of signal boxes and could appreciate the oddity of the swinging cabin above the canal on the Severn bridge, and it was not long before I had invited myself inside.

Such was the scale of the bridge that from our moorings the cabin above the swinging span looked very small. The first time, however, that I laboriously scaled the iron steps and entered it I was amazed to find it was big enough to house the two sets of horizontal steam engines and boilers (one in service and one standby) that supplied the power to semi-rotate the bridge upon its massive central pier of masonry. The keeper of the bridge doubled the roles of engine man and signalman; besides the controls for the two steam engines, he had under his hand a small lever frame of orthodox railway type. In this, one lever released the bridge locks and was controlled by the block system for the section between Sharpness and Severn Bridge station on the further side of the river. This precaution meant that the bridge could not be opened without the sanction of the signalman at each end of the section. Another lever worked an orthodox railway semaphore signal mounted above the roof of the cabin: when pulled 'off' it indicated to approaching ships that the bridge was about to swing. The two remaining levers operated railway stop signals in each direction; because there could obviously be no direct connection between these and the frame, they were worked through push rods and rocking levers. Herein lay a further safeguard, for when the bridge was swung the push rods ceased to connect with the rockers and the signals would rise to danger by the weight of their levers even if the levers in the frame were 'off'.

We crossed the bridge in the Lydney 'push-and-pull' several times during our stay for explorations in the Forest of Dean. Strangely enough, although so much of my life had been spent within easy range of it, I had visited the Forest on only one occasion and then only briefly. Our most memorable excursion was the perfect summer day when we went to Cinderford by train (this involved two changes, at Lydney and Awre Junction) and then walked the long-forsaken roadbed of the old Forest of Dean Central Railway through the heart of the Forest and thence via a still used mineral line back to Lydney and a train home. There turned out to be quite a long tunnel on the latter and we had brought no torch. After the dazzling sunlight the darkness of the tunnel was Stygian. I was walking in the four-foot, trying to measure my stride to suit the invisible sleeper spacing while Angela followed behind me when suddenly some *thing* rose up from beneath my feet and made off into the darkness. I had recently written a ghost story about a tunnel and now it seemed to be coming true. To say we were startled would be an understatement. Not until we neared the farther portal did we discover that it was a sheep which had evidently gone into the tunnel to shelter from the heat.

We found the Victorian pubs of Sharpness rather depressing. They called themselves hotels and had large unwelcoming bars smelling of a mixture of floor polish and stale beer which appeared to anticipate a volume of trade which had never materialized. Entire ships' crews? Charabanc parties? Entrants. in fishing competitions? So whenever we felt like an evening stroll and a drink we headed along the canal towpath towards the small village pub at Purton which we found very much more congenial. Judging from the company usually to be found in the bar, the male inhabitants were all either salmon fishermen or bargemen or both, people who made Purton as organic a part of the great river as an otter's holt. Often when the tide was out we would see from our moorings, far out across the estuary, these Purton salmon fishermen with their lave nets at the ready. The net was outspread between the slender ash arms or 'rimes' of a Y-shaped framework so that, as the men bore it forward, they looked like strange black insects with long antennae, crawling and questing across that waste of sand. Like Harry Rogers, many miles upstream, these men had drunk Severn water with their mother's milk; no stranger would venture so far out on these treacherous sands which the tides overwhelm with terrifying stealth and swiftness.

On the other side of the river they seemed to prefer a variant of lave net fishing. In this, the 'rimes' that spread the net were crossed over the gunwale of a boat held offshore by a steel cable and a ground anchor. We could see two of these 'stopping boats', as they are called, at work in Wellhouse Bay where the railway ran along the shore line immediately opposite our mooring. This method of fishing called for as much skill and judgement as the other, for a stopping boat with its heavy net can easily be overwhelmed by a strong flood tide. It was obvious to us that, like the putcheon weirs, these traditional methods of netting salmon were doomed to disappear. All the fishermen we met were elderly men and it was obvious that they were the last of countless generations. All complained of a dwindling salmon population which they put down to the untreated filth spewed out by Gloucester's sewers. Because of the length of the estuary, this could not escape readily but was washed to and fro by successive tides, forming a lethal barrier which the salmon could not pass. A few got through, but many more perished with the result that fewer and fewer fish came up the river to spawn. Upriver, as I knew, other hazards lay in wait for them. Harry Rogers had told me how, at times when the river was very low, dozens of dead fish would come to the surface of Severn in the neighbourhood of Ironbridge. Harry believed, correctly I think, that at such times the hot condensate from Buildwas power station raised the temperature in the river to a point at which the fish were suffocated.

During this month at Sharpness we welcomed other visitors on board besides our ancient mariner. One of these was my cousin Bill Willans who had been recently demobbed from the Navy. As readers of the first volume of this autobiography will remember, he had played a large part in my earlier life, but it was twelve years since I had last seen him. Then there was Peter Scott, recently installed in the farmhouse at the nearby New Grounds which was to be the headquarters of his Wild Fowl Trust. Finally, there was the late Brian Waters from

Cirencester to whom I had written, inviting him to come over. If Angela had not given me his book *Severn Tide* as a Christmas present it is unlikely that we should have taken *Cressy* to Sharpness at all. I am glad I was able to extend hospitality to this gentle, modest, soft-spoken man and to thank him personally for having written such a splendid book. Though its author died untimely, *Severn Tide* still stands as the best book ever written – or likely to be written – about the tidal Severn and the country beside it. To read it is to understand how it captivated us and why the month we passed at Sharpness fled by all too soon. The visit had no motive so far as the I.W.A. was concerned, and in this sense it was a pure holiday. But now it was otherwise and so, regretfully, we slipped our moorings and headed northwards, our ultimate destination being Stone on the Trent & Mersey canal in Staffordshire.

I had no first-hand experience of the canals of northern England, nor had anyone else in the I.W.A. at that time, so Robert Aickman and I decided to embark upon a joint cruise over these unknown waters. It was, however, out of the question to use *Cressy* because she would be too long for the locks. On the 'Keel canals' of Yorkshire, for example, the locks are only 57ft 6in. long, which means that it is impossible to design a 'go-anywhere' craft without sacrificing a considerable amount of living space. So we decided to charter, although at that time suitable craft were not exactly thick on the water. Before the war there had only been one boat hirer on the entire narrow canal system and now there were two. The newcomer was R. H. Wyatt who, with his son, had set up in business at the old wharf and dock at Stone. When he was first fired with this idea, Wyatt had come to see me at Tardebigge and I remember being somewhat torn – and by no means for the last time – between my desire to find traffic of any kind that would help to keep the canals alive and my conscience in encouraging a man to take what I knew to be an extremely risky step. Even if Wyatt could find enough customers, and that was problematical, it was even more doubtful if he could find enough boats, while he lacked both the capital and the experience to design and build his own fleet.

There were then very few boats suitable for cruising on the

canals. The most popular form of pleasure boat on the inland
waterways was a converted ship's lifeboat such as the *Miranda*
which Angela and I had hired on the Lower Avon before the war.
But almost invariably such craft were too beamy to pass through
the locks of narrow canals. Nevertheless, Wyatt did succeed in
acquiring a motley and dubious collection of boats which always
seemed to be either breaking down or sinking. Their condition
soon became so bad that they were unfit to hire and he asked
me in desperation what he could do. I suggested that he should
buy two old butty boats from S. E. Barlow, a canal carrier
friend of mine at Tamworth who had a boat dock, and ask him
to cut them in half and convert them into four canal cruisers.
When these four craft came into service Wyatt's boat troubles
were over, but in 1948 they were still in the future and we had
agreed to charter from him for our northern voyage the *Ailsa
Craig* which was by repute the best of his original bad lot. I
think her hull had once been an exceptionally slim ship's lifeboat, but that must have been a long time ago because it was
very rotten. Over the details of her engine room memory has
drawn a decent veil; but I do recall that I, as the engineer of the
party, was plagued with mechanical troubles of one kind or
another. Altogether I marvel now that we were able to complete
so ambitious an itinerary. This was to travel from Stone to
Ashton-under-Lyne via the Trent & Mersey, Macclesfield,
Peak Forest and Ashton Canals and then climb from Ashton
over the Pennines by the Huddersfield Narrow Canal. As all
these waterways except the first were disused and in a pretty
deplorable state, our eventual arrival in Huddersfield was in
doubt to say the least; but assuming we did so, we then planned
to aim for Leeds via the Calder & Hebble and Aire & Calder
Navigations, and then to re-cross the Pennines to Wigan and
Leigh by the Leeds & Liverpool Canal. The final leg which
completed the circuit would be the historic Bridgewater Canal
from Leigh to Preston Brook, and thence back to Stone by the
Trent & Mersey.

This venture was to be essayed by a crew of four, and because
of the limited space on *Ailsa Craig* we decided to put on board
a small tent and two sleeping bags, the idea being that we
should take it in turns to sleep afloat or ashore. By the time

Cressy, reached R. H. Wyatt's wharf at Stone on 11 August, *Ailsa Craig* had already left with a full complement on board, the idea being that when they reached the summit level of the Huddersfield Narrow Canal at Diggle, on the Lancashire side of the Pennines, they would send us a signal whereupon we would travel by rail to Diggle station. I was determined not to miss what might be the last opportunity to travel through Britain's longest canal tunnel, over three miles long from Diggle to Marsden, on the highest summit level – 644ft 9in. above sea level to be exact. The couple we were replacing were likewise determined not to miss this unique experience, so it was agreed that they would leave from Marsden station beside the Yorkshire mouth of the tunnel. This meant that for her subterranean passage under the Pennines, *Ailsa Craig* would have a crew of six which, as things turned out, was just as well.

We lay at Stone Wharf for twelve days before the long awaited signal came and we set off for Diggle. The reason for this delay was that, despite *Ailsa Craig*'s shallow draught, for most of the way the bottom was too near the top, particularly on the Ashton Canal where the bottom consisted mainly of scrap metal which had been tipped into the canal over the years. Her crew had had the most frightful trouble hereabouts, but they had survived it and had climbed the long ladder of locks leading to the summit so that as our train ran into Diggle station we could see *Ailsa Craig* moored just outside the mouth of the tunnel.

Many canal tunnels appear to have been driven without sufficient reason as though, like the builder of some model garden railway, the engineer had said, 'Let's have a tunnel'. The explanation is that the early canal engineers would rather tunnel than excavate a deep cutting because the amount of spoil to be handled was less. But here it was quite otherwise. Straight ahead of us rose the sooty-green flank of Standedge quartered with blackened dry stone walls. Beneath it; the black hole of the canal tunnel looked no bigger than a mouse-hole in a wainscot. Our passage through it was one of the most eerie and sensational experiences of my life. Begun in the last years of the eighteenth century, the driving of the tunnel took twelve years. It was a seemingly endless battle between man and stubborn rock fought by dim candle light in the bowels of the Pennines. One reason why it took so long was that the height above was so great that few working shafts were driven; even so, one of these, left open for ventilation, is 600ft deep. The tunnellers did have one bonus, however – the rock was so hard and free from faults that there was no need for any lining. Hence it resembled a natural cavern rather than a man-made tunnel. This resemblance was heightened by the great variations in the diameter of the bore. It appeared to me that whenever the miners had encountered rock of soft or doubtful quality they had cut it back until they found a safe roof; it was difficult otherwise to account for the fact that a tunnel of the minimum width of 7ft 6in. (officially) and only 8ft 6in. above water level would, every now and again, open out to such cavernous proportions. There was, of course, no towing path and such great variations in size must have made it extremely difficult to propel the boats through the tunnel. Traffic was operated on the 'one-way' principle and, according to de Salis in his famous *Guide*, boats were 'legged' through. In that case, I came to the conclusion, the boatmen of those days must have had telescopic legs.

The passage of the tunnel must have taken us at least two hours for we took it extremely slowly. The jagged rocks on either side looked peculiarly menacing and I was only too well aware that, instead of *Cressy*'s two-inch oak planking, there was only half an inch of rotten wood in our hull. In the narrow places, contact with the rock was unavoidable and in one of these *Ailsa Craig* stuck fast. As we had just about reached the middle of the tunnel by this time, it was not a situation calculated to appeal to sufferers from claustrophobia. The trouble was that *Ailsa Craig*'s hull was the wrong shape for the job. Instead of being almost straight-sided like a narrow boat and with cabin sides tumbling home from the gunwales, her hull flared outwards from the water and this line had been continued through to the top corners of her cabin work. It was true that her beam nowhere exceeded 7 feet, but 7 feet at a height of about 4ft 6in. above water level was too much for the low arch of the roof. I was reminded of the situation the previous year when *Cressy* had stuck in the lock at Grindley Brook and it seemed to call for equally drastic measures. It was fortunate that there were six of us on board, for not only had this brought the boat lower in the water but it spelled that much more man-power, which might well be needed in a situation such as this. Fortunately, too, the jagged walls of the tunnel provided plenty of purchase in our efforts to free the boat. These efforts were not helped by the atmosphere which was as thick and sulphurous as the infernal regions due to the presence of cross-galleries at intervals connecting the canal tunnel to the parallel railway tunnels on each side. These galleries had been driven by the railway engineers in lieu of working shafts. From their point of view the canal engineers may have laboured in vain, but they certainly made things much easier for their successors. As we struggled in the choking darkness to free *Ailsa Craig* an occasional thunderous reverberation followed by a fresh blast of smoke signified the passage of a train.

At length our boat floated freely astern. There was only room to crawl between the roof of the cabin and the low vault of the tunnel, but by lying on our stomachs we contrived to prise off the wooden rubbing strake which extended along each side at cabin roof level. Had the boat not been so rotten, this would have been a much more difficult and brutal operation. As it was, it was soon done and gained us about an inch and a half overall which, in the event, made the vital difference between go and no go. Having got the strakes off, the only course was to drive *Ailsa Craig* full ahead into the narrow place in the hope that she would go through – which, with a certain amount of creaking protest, she did. Fortunately, we encountered no further similar obstacle until eventually we glimpsed, through the murky darkness ahead, the wan arc of daylight that marked the Marsden or Yorkshire end of the tunnel. Slowly the light ahead grew larger and brighter until at last we emerged, blinking, into the late afternoon sunlight.

Ailsa Craig was not the last boat to pass through Standedge Tunnel. Some years after the closure of the canal, British Waterways continued to run special trips through it for societies and parties interested in such things. But I think we may well have been the last boat to travel through the whole twenty miles of waterway from Ashton to Huddersfield, and it would be true to say that by this time the canal was only just navigable, the chief trouble being at the locks. When a canal falls into disuse, the locks are left empty so that, in the case of most narrow canals, it is not the small single upper gates of the locks but the deeper double lower gates which are the first to fail. As the months and years pass with no water against them, they dry out, shrink, crack and finally rot. In this case there were no less than seventy-four pairs of lower gates that needed replacing, for the Huddersfield Narrow Canal is little more than a ladder of locks, its summit, most of it in tunnel, being the longest level pound. And at each of these locks it was a matter of anxious concern whether the water entering the lock chamber through the upper paddles could overcome the amount that was leaking out through the lower gates. It was like trying to fill a bath with the plug out. The most critical moment came shortly after we left the east end of Standedge Tunnel and began the long descent to Huddersfield. A friendly and helpful lengthman from Marsden went ahead along the towpath to fill the locks ready for us. He had filled one of these locks when a sizeable portion of one of the lower gates blew out under the pressure of water. He had previously opened the top gate ready to admit us. Fortunately *Ailsa Craig* was already inside the chamber and we had begun to swing the top gate shut behind her when it happened, otherwise we might have had to beat an ignominious retreat. As it was, the top gate swung shut with a resounding crash by which time the water level had already dropped a foot. I have never seen a boat sink more swiftly in a lock chamber. I doubt if that lock gate was ever made good, for not long after our passage concrete weirs replaced the top gates at every lock so that never again would anyone travel in our wake.

Angela and I spent that night in the tent. It was for us a novel experience and we both resolved that, when this trip was over, it was one which neither of us would ever repeat. I write 'spent' rather than 'slept' advisedly. It was one of those small tents that you enter on all fours like a dog going into a kennel. We pitched it, not without difficulty, in a meadow that sloped down to the north bank of the canal midway between Marsden and Huddersfield. To anyone interested in the history of industrial England, the narrow valleys of the Pennines have tremendous character and atmosphere, but at the same time they make bleak and forbidding camp sites. This valley was no exception. Opposite, across the canal, a high straight-topped ridge of moorland enclosed it, and against this background there marched a succession of mill chimneys, each breathing a gentle fume of smoke from boiler fires banked against the morrow. About the feet of these tall spires consecrated to industry were the mill buildings and the little communities of mill workers: Slaithwaite, Linthwaite and Golcar. There were also some small scattered farms, their houses and buildings so low-browed that they seemed to crouch against the bitter east winds that funnelled up the valley. And everything, walls, factories and farms alike, was built of stone that looked as if it had been blackened by centuries of smoke. It must have been a wild and primitive country before the mills came. Now it was neither town nor country; yet, so far from civilizing it, the presence of the mills with their gaunt stacks seemed to make it more savage.

Although it had been a sunny day, by nightfall it had clouded over and this made the prospect of a night under canvas in such surroundings even less inviting. With great difficulty we undressed, insinuated ourselves into the narrow camp beds and then turned out the portable gas light. Hardly had we done so when rain began to patter on the canvas just above our heads, making sleep impossible. The tent began to stir uneasily in the wind that came with the rain, and then to sway more vigorously. There were unmistakable sounds from outside which indicated that a herd of bullocks was examining closely and curiously the alien object which had appeared in its pasture. I was well aware of the rule against pitching tents in fields with livestock in them and before dark I had satisfied myself, as I thought, that there were no such animals. I can only suppose I had failed to spot that our field was open to another from which they had now come to plague us. They blundered into the guy ropes and it was soon obvious that if they were not chased away we should be enveloped in the damp canvas ruin of our tent. Torch in hand, bare feet thrust into shoes and with a mackintosh over my pyjamas I crawled out into the night and

put the invaders to flight. It was pouring with rain, not verti-
cally but horizontally, and I had to spend some time squelching
about retrieving uprooted tent pegs, driving them in again
with a mallet and replacing and adjusting guy ropes. All night
long the rain teemed down and ever and anon I had to make
further forays outside to stampede the cattle. Our tent was
unlined and one piece of camping lore I had picked up was that
if you pressed against wet canvas from the inside the rain would
come through at that point. Since no one who was not a practised
contortionist could avoid doing this in our tent, it soon became
almost as wet inside as it was out, and little rivulets of water
trickled over our ground-sheet as they made their way down
the gentle slope. It was a most blessed relief when the rain
ceased at first light and the sun rose. We had many more
uncomfortable nights in that tent before the voyage was over,
but never again, I am thankful to say, quite such a baptism of
flood.

In theory, at least, *Cressy* could have carried us thus far but
little farther; at Huddersfield she would have had to return by
the way she had come. For Lancastrians and Yorkists had
different ideas about canal gauges, the former favouring narrow
boats and the latter Yorkshire keels which are short but broad
of beam. So it came about that at Huddersfield our canal made
an end-on junction with the Huddersfield Broad Canal which is
virtually a short branch of the Calder & Hebble Navigation and,
like the latter, has locks less than sixty feet long. Consequently
only minuscule boats that were both narrow and short could use
this waterway as a through route. This is one of the more crazy
results of the fact that the English waterway system, if such it
can be called, was the product of many local undertakings, each
considered in isolation at the time of construction.

When we had passed through Huddersfield and reached the
Calder & Hebble it was a relief to find ourselves in well
frequented waters once again. As we dropped down the locks
towards the junction of the Aire & Calder Navigation at Fall
Ing, near Wakefield, we passed a number of commercial craft,
mostly timber-built Yorkshire keels with diesel engines in
place of their original square sails. It would be the same now
for the rest of the journey so that, provided *Ailsa Craig* could be

kept going and did not sink, we should complete the circuit. Certain things seen on that journey have stayed in my memory, such as the unexpected sight of an ex-Leeds & Liverpool Canal Carrying Company steamer which we overhauled on the Aire & Calder as it was puffing energetically towards Castleford Junction with a cargo of coal.

The broad reaches of the Aire & Calder Navigation approaching Leeds were memorable because they were the most polluted waters I had ever seen. It was like boating through black ink. In such depths nothing could live and what, at a distance, looked like a heavy rise of fish proved to be great bubbles of foul gas rising from the bottom to break upon the surface. I remember the climb of the Leeds & Liverpool Canal up Airedale, culminating in the sensational 'five-rise' lock at Bingley; and then the long, winding level of seventeen miles through the Yorkshire countryside and the market town of Skipton to Gargrave bottom lock. Of the long descent into Lancashire from Foulridge summit tunnel, it is the crossing of the long and high embankment at Burnley that stays in my mind. The view it afforded over Burnley with its many smoking mill chimneys was surely one of the most remarkable industrial landscapes in Britain, and certainly not one you might expect to see from a boat. I have never been back to Burnley and I suspect that developers have now transformed its old, gritty, dramatic, nineteenth-century self into a featureless concrete jungle. Better a bad character than no character at all.

Back in narrow boat waters, I remember exploring that birthplace of the English canals, Worsley Basin, and my excitement at finding, still afloat there, one of the 'starvationers' – the small, slim craft that were used to navigate the underground canal system leading to the 'Canal Duke's' collieries. Shortly after this, as we approached the Barton Swing Aqueduct, a cargo steamer was coming up the Manchester Ship Canal which gave us a memorable opportunity of seeing at close quarters the hydraulic doors closed against us and then this most remarkable device begin to swing, water, towpath and all. From this point, one long level of the Bridgewater Canal took us to the junction of the Trent & Mersey Canal at Preston Brook, and so through many tunnels and by Middlewich and Stoke-on-Trent back to

Stone wharf where we arrived on the evening of 17 September.

Although it had been such a memorable experience, how glad we both were to be home again aboard *Cressy* after those cramped quarters on *Ailsa Craig*, not to mention that terrible tent! After a couple of days laying in stores we were under way once more, heading south again via Fradley and Hawkesbury Junctions to reach our winter quarters at Banbury on a fine and frosty evening at the beginning of October. Since she had left Banbury in April, *Cressy* had covered 346 miles. By modern motoring standards this is a trivial distance, but it is not so trivial when, snail-like, you are carrying your house around with you at a steady 3 m.p.h.

Chapter 7

Pont Cysyllte – An Ambition Achieved

In spite of our defeat in 1947, I had by no means abandoned my seventeen-year-old ambition to take *Cressy* over the Vale of Llangollen by the Pont Cysyllte Aqueduct. For the old boat it would be in the nature of a homecoming after who knows how many years of wandering, for it was in a dock beside the north end of this aqueduct that she had been built just before the First World War. From our previous experience it was obvious that it would be pointless to make a second attempt on the Welsh Canal until the new flowmeter installation at Llantisilio had been completed and a reliable water supply assured. This was one reason why we had made Sharpness our objective the previous summer. But, with the coming of spring, encouraging reports from Wales made us determine to try again; so 21 May 1949 found us heading north from Banbury once more. As on the previous occasion two years before, we travelled via the northern end of the Stratford Canal. The G.W.R. had been nationalized in the meantime and we thought it would be a good idea to remind the canal's new owners of their obligations. This time we experienced only minor difficulties and arrived at King's Norton to find the infamous Lifford bridge jacked up to ample height, while the shoal of ashes which had almost filled the canal beyond had been cleared away. At the junction with the Worcester & Birmingham Canal, instead of turning left for Tardebigge and the Severn as we had done on previous occasions, we turned north towards Birmingham because this time I was anxious to head for the Welsh Border as quickly as possible and the shortest water route thither lay through the Black Country.

We moored that night beneath the trees a little to the south of the short Edgbaston tunnel, a remarkably secluded and peaceful place considering we were no more than a mile from the centre of the city. The only noise was made by the trains that passed by on the old Midland main line to the west which runs parallel with the canal hereabouts. Although the sound of motor traffic has lost me much sleep, trains have never disturbed me; in fact I love the sight and sound of them – particularly when they are steam-hauled as they were in 1949. I remember once about this period I deliberately moored *Cressy* for the night on the Oxford Canal at a point near Brinklow where it runs close beside the Euston–Crewe main line for the sheer pleasure of seeing the Night Scot and the Irish Mail come pounding past my windows at close range.

The route we had now chosen was not only much shorter but it saved us a great deal of lockage. In the fifteen miles of canal to Wolverhampton there were only three locks and I reckoned that if we made a fairly prompt start next day we should reach the Shropshire Union Canal main line before night fell. To anyone like myself over whom the early relics of England's industrial revolution exercised a curious fascination, part aesthetic, part dramatic and part horrific, travelling by canal through an urban and industrial area twenty-five years ago was an uniquely rewarding experience. I have mentioned the view of industrial Burnley from the Leeds & Liverpool Canal, and in *Narrow Boat* I described what it was like to travel by the Trent & Mersey Canal through the Potteries with their thickly smoking ovens, and through the heart of the Shelton Steelworks. To voyage through the Black Country by the main line of the Birmingham Canal Navigations was another rewarding and memorable experience. On either hand were visual reminders of that earliest industrial England which the canals had helped to create. Although it was ringed by areas of later growth brought about by rail and road transport, this old blackened core still survived and was, in many cases, still alive and still using the canal as its life-line. All this was particularly true of the Black Country and its complicated network of canals. The 'B.C.N.' was certainly very much alive the day that we passed through. Not only were there many long-distance motor boats and their butties, but also a great number of short-haul 'day-boats', some towed in trains by tugs but the majority horsedrawn.

Nevertheless, despite the fascination the Black Country then held for me, we decided not to spend a night in it but to press on through it if only because the waters of its canals were so grossly polluted. Such is the complexity of the Black Country canal network that this was the only occasion on the whole of my canal voyaging when I almost took a wrong turning. Shortly after we had locked up to the Wolverhampton level at Tipton and were approaching Bloomfield Junction, my sense of direction played me false and we should have sailed off down what is called the Wednesbury Oak Loop Line had not a friendly local character on the towpath set me right by shouting and pointing in the direction of Coseley tunnel. Had we taken this wrong turning we should eventually have rejoined our route at the expense of four extra, winding miles of canal, for this so-called loop line, like other similar diversions, was a part of the original tortuous main line of canal between Birmingham and Wolverhampton. The completion of Coseley tunnel in 1837 had led to the disuse of the loop by through traffic. Although it is only 360 yards long, we had never been through a canal tunnel of such princely proportions. Coseley's height above water level is over fifteen feet, while its overall width of nearly twenty-five feet is sufficient to allow for a towing path on each side. These dimensions were only later surpassed by the nearby Netherton Tunnel, the last to be built in England.

At Coseley we were only three miles from Wolverhampton and evening found us descending the flight of twenty-one locks that brings the Birmingham Canal down to the level of the Staffordshire & Worcestershire Canal at Aldersley Junction, a mere half mile away from Autherley where the Shropshire Union Canal begins. Some people think this canal from Wolverhampton to Nantwich boring because its course is so straight compared with the windings of the older contour canals. I never found it so. I admired the boldness of its engineering and the sense of spaciousness that this boldness imparted. I loved the wide pastoral landscapes that unfolded as one's boat slid out from the green shades of some deep cutting on to a lofty embankment. Here the only enemy was the wind; on the embankments it could be so strong that a boat drawing little water and carrying much 'top' was no longer able to go forward. In the attempt to counter such a cross-wind I would put *Cressy* full ahead and bring her bows into the wind. This meant that we progressed in a crab-wise fashion until the stern was on the mud on one side of the canal and the bows in the bank on the other. When this happened there was nothing to be done but shut our engine off and call it a day. On this occasion, however, we enjoyed calm weather and, despite stops for supplies and to pick up a visitor at Market Drayton and Nantwich, on the morning of Sunday 5 June we swung on to the Welsh Canal once more at Hurleston Junction.

With vivid memories of the many difficulties we had encountered on the previous occasion, we now went ahead with caution mingled with some trepidation, wondering especially what would happen when we came to that tight lock chamber at Grindley Brook. We need not have worried, for the improvement that had taken place in two years was quite remarkable, considering that the canal had been officially abandoned and no one was under compulsion to do anything to assist navigation. There was more water, less weed and fewer scours of mud from tributary streams. The villainous one at Blackoe Cottages, which had caused us so much trouble before, seemed to have disappeared. Most miraculous of all, work must have been done on the masonry of the lock sides and wing-walls, for we sailed up the flight at Grindley Brook with no trouble at all.

When the railway-owned canals were transferred to the Docks & Inland Waterways Executive, generally speaking the new masters proved very little better than the old, and they were certainly less accountable to Parliament for their actions. But in the case of the Welsh Canal the good fairy was Christopher Marsh, engineer for the North-Western Division and the only member of the senior staff of the new Executive who had canal water in his veins. At this time, the greatest threat to this waterway was that the highway overbridges would be lowered. Since the canal had been abandoned for navigation, the county highway authorities were no longer under any legal obligation to maintain navigable headroom. This threat took formidable shape about this time when the proposal was made to remove the awkward dog-leg bridge carrying the A539 Ruabon–Llangollen road over the canal at Brynmelyn and replace it by a culverted embankment. It was pleasant indeed to find Christopher Marsh on our side in the battle over this bridge, arguing that the waterway could only be maintained in a safe condition by water, and therefore there must be sufficient headroom for his maintenance boats to pass.

It was thanks to this change in the official attitude towards the Welsh Canal that our voyage to Ellesmere and beyond was so enjoyable, and so uneventful compared with the previous occasion. Nevertheless it was only by luck that this third attempt to reach Pont Cysyllte was not again frustrated. A chance visit to the pub at Bettisfield where we had moored for the night, followed by a conversation with a local farmer, gave us the information that a new water pipeline from Vrynwy reservoir was shortly to be laid across the canal at the village of Hindford, which meant that it would be blocked by a coffer dam for an indefinite period. I was determined not to be beaten a third time, even if it meant spending the winter in Wales, so we decided to press on and get *Cressy* past the point of obstruction before work started.

We only paused at Ellesmere for shopping followed by a brief picnic lunch before entering waters which had been unnavigable before but which were now almost weed-free. Soon we passed the junction with the derelict Montgomeryshire Canal and in another two miles came to the site of the new pipeline works just before the canal entered the village of Hindford, where we moored up about 6 p.m. It was over this length of canal that *Cressy* had run her first steam trial after conversion at Mr Beech's dock beside the locks at Frankton just twenty years before, and now she was revisiting it for the first time. In the interval, both the boatyard and the locks beside it had fallen to ruin. Just before the war, a burst in the canal bank near Lockgate Bridge, a little distance below Frankton Locks, had provided the L.M. & S.R. with a welcome pretext to abandon the thirty-five miles of canal that followed the Severn down the Welsh Border to Newtown. His occupation gone, Beech the boatbuilder went to work as a carpenter on a new

R.A.F. airfield near Oswestry; how I heard that he was now retired and living in Hindford I do not remember, but we sought him out and invited the old man and his wife on board for a drink and a talk. He took a wholly unfeigned and unselfconscious delight in seeing so unexpectedly this past product of his craftsmanship. To see this old boatbuilder seated in one of our armchairs, his gnarled hands grasped in his lap and beaming with pleasure, was alone worth the trip.

Next morning as we left Hindford and passed through the two locks at New Marton – the only locks west of Grindley Brook – it soon became apparent that no craft of *Cressy*'s size and draught had penetrated so far for many years. Progress became very slow. Numerous small scours from incoming streams had built up over the years, so that once again I had to put our pulley blocks to use to force a way through them. But these were only minor troubles and not to be compared with those we had experienced two years before. This is rather a dull stretch of canal. It winds through a somewhat flat and nondescript landscape and St Martins is unashamedly a colliery village, an untidy brick sprawl which might have been translated from Durham and dumped amid the green fields of Shropshire. But at Chirk Bank the Welsh Canal springs yet another of its landscape surprises. Closely accompanied by Telford's Holyhead Road, Telford's canal takes a sudden swing to the westward and soon we found ourselves looking down into the valley of the Ceiriog which here forms the boundary between England and Wales. Whereas the road swoops down to the valley bottom to cross the Ceiriog at low level, the canal clings to the contour high above until it turns north once more to stride across the river and its valley on Telford's splendid aqueduct of stone. With its ten spans and a maximum height of seventy feet, Chirk aqueduct is one of the major canal engineering works in England, and it would be more celebrated were it not for the proximity of its greater neighbour at Pont Cysyllte. As *Cressy* glided across the aqueduct, standing at the tiller I looked westward between the arches of the parallel railway viaduct at the green floor of the valley beneath the hanging woods of Chirk Castle park and thought nostalgically of childhood visits to Plas y Garth at Glynceiriog, rattling up the valley by a Glyn

Valley Tramway that had now vanished without trace. How much of my life had been associated in one way or another with the Welsh Marches and how powerful had been their effect upon me. *Cressy* herself had been built there and now, under my hand, she was being attracted back as the needle of a compass is attracted to the north.

The river Ceiriog hereabouts forms the boundary between Shropshire and Denbighshire and I know of no more dramatic entry to Wales than by Telford's Chirk aqueduct and the tunnel that immediately follows it. Because the hills of the north, or Welsh, side of the Vale of Ceiriog are higher than those to the south, there is only room for a basin at the north end of the aqueduct before the canal dives underground. It was in this basin, poised between hill and vale, that we moored for the night, feeling that now, for the first time, we really were in Wales – that brief excursion into 'Flintshire detached' seemed a political accident which did not really count.

Chirk Tunnel is just over a quarter of a mile long and was one of the first to be constructed with a towpath through it. Telford was a humane man who considered that the practice of 'legging' boats through tunnels degraded man to a mere beast of burden whereas his predecessors and contemporaries had no such scruples. The price of the towpath at Chirk is that it is a 'one way' tunnel, but we slipped into it next morning with no anxiety whatever, for on this pioneering voyage there was not the slightest prospect of meeting traffic coming the other way. The Shrewsbury to Chester line of the old G.W.R. crosses over Chirk Tunnel so that although the railway viaduct had been on our left hand as we crossed the aqueduct, when we emerged from the tunnel into a long tree-shaded cutting, Chirk Station lay to the right of us. We took this cutting extremely slowly and warily, for its waters were exceptionally shallow, and beneath the surface we glimpsed water-logged tree-branches here and there. Our progress was made slower by the fact that there was a perceptible current in the canal due to its function as a feeder to Hurleston reservoir. This became particularly noticeable in such shallow places where *Cressy's* hull virtually became a moving barrage.

On the right hand at the end of the cutting is Black Park

basin, now choked with reeds and mud but once a scene of
great activity during the heyday of the Shropshire Union Canal
Carrying Company. Here coal was brought from neighbouring
collieries to be loaded into boats, and here also an extension of
the Glyn Valley Tramway from Chirk Station brought for
transhipment slate and granite roadstone from quarries at
Glynceiriog and on the road to Llanarmon near the headwaters
of the Ceiriog. A mile beyond Black Park we passed beneath
Telford's Holyhead road by the second and much shorter tunnel
called Whitehouses or Whitehurst. The next bridge beyond
the tunnel is called Irish Bridge and so probably perpetuates
the memory of the many Irish labourers who helped to build the
canal, tramping across Wales from Holyhead. Here the canal
again swings sharply to the west and crosses the line of Offa's
Dyke to enter the Vale of Llangollen. As we approached the
village of Vron Cysyllte we could see away to our right the tall
stone piers of the aqueduct that carries the canal across the
Dee.

We could have crossed the aqueduct that day, but instead we
tied up at what had once been the village wharf at 'the Vron',
as the locals call it, but is now disused and grass-grown. The
canal widens into a small basin at this point for it was once its
temporary terminus while the great aqueduct was still building.
We decided to stop at Vron Wharf for two reasons, first because
Angela was due in London on the morrow and secondly to await
the coming of Hugh Griffith, the Welsh actor, and his wife
Gunde who were coming to stay with us for a week and were
anxious to share with us the experience of crossing Pont
Cysyllte by boat.

My career as a writer has brought me too many correspondents and a number of acquaintances but few lasting friendships.
Of the latter I can think of only four whom I would never have
otherwise met. One of these was Charles Hadfield and another
was Hugh Griffith. Charles had written to me when *Narrow
Boat* was first published but Hugh, curiously enough, was
attracted by *High Horse Riderless*. Hugh and Gunde were staying
with friends in the village of Sibford Gower near Banbury early
in 1949 when Hugh discovered quite by chance through a
mutual acquaintance that I was then living at Tooley's Boatyard.

As a result, Angela and I motored out to Sibford to meet them. From that moment our friendship grew rapidly and over the next ten years Hugh and I saw a great deal of each other. Hugh is an Anglesey man and what I most admired in him was his intensely localized Welshness, his deep feeling for his native place, which has never been diminished or spoiled by his success. I think that what had drawn his interest in the first place was the chapter in *High Horse Riderless* in which I argued the case for the devolution of the powers of central government as one of the essential conditions for the more vigorous and self-sufficient regional society which I advocated. Although when I wrote this chapter it was with no particular district or country in mind, it was seized upon by Hugh in particular and by the Welsh Nationalist Party in general. It was with an odd mixture of gratification and embarrassment that I found myself quoted *in extenso* in the party's pamphlet arguing the case for self-government. Because it seemed to me to be trying to practise what I had preached, I felt that I could scarely do other than become a Welsh Nationalist myself. This was the only time I have joined a political party and I suppose that by doing so I became in the technical sense a traitor to my own country, but I fear it was not long before I allowed my subscription to lapse. My love has always been for that Border Country that is neither wholly English nor wholly Welsh but seems to me to combine the best of both. I was soon to become somewhat disillusioned about Welsh Wales.

It was while I was alone on *Cressy* at Vron Wharf awaiting the return of Angela and the arrival of our guests that I had an experience which, though it had a perfectly rational explanation then unknown to me, seemed so strangely dream-like and unreal at the time that the whole episode comes vividly to the mind's eye to this day. Just astern of *Cressy* was a typical Shropshire Union drawbridge of that graceful kind with overhead balance beams and dependent chains which is found in Holland and in the paintings of Van Gogh. A steep lane led down from the village to this bridge which provided access to the towpath and to the green pastures beyond, sloping down towards the Dee. It was a golden June evening and I was preparing my supper in the galley when, hearing a strange hubbub compounded of music and many voices, I ran towards the aft deck and saw to my amazement a scene that blended Van Gogh with Goya and our own Richard Wilson. Coming down the steep lane towards me was a company of Spanish dancers in full fig, followed by musicians and what looked like the entire population of Vron Cysyllte. The Spanish girls were the first to cross the wooden drawbridge; they moved with that particularly graceful swing of the hips which I had only seen before in certain young gypsy women. Their long full skirts swayed as they walked, and their lace mantillas swept back from the tall tortoiseshell combs in their dark hair. They were followed by their partners in short, black bolero jackets and tight trousers. So unlikely a sight in such surroundings it would have been difficult to conceive. If a sea serpent had suddenly swum into my ken along the canal I could scarcely have regarded it with greater incredulity than this colourful spectacle of old Castille crossing a drawbridge not thirty yards away. When the whole procession had crossed the bridge, the villagers formed a circle on the one piece of smooth and level turf in the meadow below. Then, on this impromptu stage, with a strumming of guitars and a clicking of castanets, the Spaniards began to dance. I quickly joined the spectators. It was as though a flock of dowdy sparrows had gathered to watch with envy the courtship rituals of some exotic, dazzling species of tropical bird. The explanation, of course, was simple. I was not aware that the Llangollen International Eisteddfod was taking place the following week; nor that it had become the custom to board the foreign teams in the villages round about. Vron Cysyllte, it appeared, habitually played host to the Spaniards who, in return for this hospitality, gave the villagers a special preview of their Eisteddfod performance. Yet no such prosaic explanation could erase from recollection the impression made upon my mind by the first vivid glimpse of that extraordinary procession trooping down the hill towards me.

When Angela returned, and Hugh and Gunde had arrived, we cast off from Vron Wharf to complete the last brief but highly dramatic section of our voyage. Pont Cysyllte aqueduct is approached by an embankment which is itself an unique feat of engineering, being no less than ninety-seven feet high at its tip. With the possible exception of the prehistoric Silbury Hill, no greater earthwork so far as I know had ever been raised in Britain by that date. Its slopes are now thickly clothed with trees which conceal its height and shut off the view of the valley below. All one can see ahead as one rounds a gentle bend between this shady avenue of trees is the long, straight perspective of the iron trough. These masking trees, however, do provide an effect of dramatic surprise, as I realized when *Cressy* slid out from their shade straight on to the towering aqueduct. On the east side is the towpath with its elegant iron railing, but on the west there is only the rim of the trough standing about six inches above water level, so that from my position at the tiller I had an uninterrupted view up the Vale of Llangollen towards the ancient Welsh fortress of Castell Dynas Bran that guards the little town. On this brilliant, cloudless June day, the valley floor was most richly green while the more distant hills basked in a shimmering blue haze of heat. In the foreground a game of cricket was in progress on the smooth, carefully tended turf of the local sports field, and I found myself looking directly down at the little, white, foreshortened figures as they crouched tense or, at a distant cry of 'Come on!', scuttled between the wickets.

This panorama, thus suddenly disclosed, was breathtaking, particularly when combined with the slow, gliding motion of a boat which one automatically associates with lush and level water-meadows, willow trees and browsing cattle. No wonder the romantic writers and artists of the early nineteenth century were united in their praise of the engineer:

> TELFORD who o'er the vale of Cambrian Dee
> Aloft in air at giddy height upborne
> Carried his Navigable road . . .

wrote Robert Southey. For engineering was then rightly considered by artist and engineer alike as an art rather than a science, and Pont Cysyllte aqueduct provided precisely that dramatic contrast between the art of man and natural beauty that they most admired, using such adjectives as 'awful' or 'sublime'. As, with *Cressy*'s engine slowed to a tick-over, we crept out on to the aqueduct, I found myself in complete sympathy with their ardour. It was an experience well worth the years of waiting and the repeated frustrations before we had been able, at last, to win through. I think we were one of the first boats, and certainly the first narrow boat, to cross Pont Cysyllte for at least ten years and I wished there had been somebody with a camera down below amongst the cricketers to record the event. But players and spectators alike were too absorbed in their game even to notice *Cressy's* slow passing high overhead. Perhaps they had assumed too readily that such boats would come that way no more.

Since there was no one below to record this historic occasion – historic for me anyway – Angela stepped out on to the towpath with her camera. As *Cressy* was almost as wide as the trough, there was really no need for me to steer so, leaving the engine running slow ahead, I went forward to join the others on the foredeck while *Cressy* drifted slowly along on to the highest portion of the aqueduct where, as I sat on the gunwale, there was nothing below me but the waters of the Dee hurrying over rapids 127 feet below.

People often ask why such prodigious engineering works were ever undertaken merely to bring water transport to the small Welsh town of Llangollen. On the face of it, it certainly seems excessively optimistic even for the brief 'canal mania' years of the 1790s. The answer is that the canal was intended to run due north from Pont Cysyllte, climbing by locks to a summit level not far from the famous John Wilkinson's flourishing ironworks and Brymbo and Bersham, thus tapping the traffic of the Wrexham coal and iron district before descending by the valley of the little river Alyn to Chester and so on to Ellesmere Port. As a result of the changed conditions brought about by the Napoleonic War, the fortunes of the Ellesmere Canal Company withered and this part of its projected main line was never built; and because of this, the rest of the canal was deprived of its intended summit water supply. It was to remedy this deficiency that the canal from Pont Cysyllte to Llangollen and Llantisilio was built in the form of a navigable feeder. It is terraced along the northern slopes of the Vale of Llangollen and joins what was to have been the main line at right angles almost immediately after the end of the aqueduct.

Because of the difficult terrain, and since its primary function was to act as a feeder, this section of the canal is unusually narrow. At the time of which I am writing, its effective width was made even narrower by the amount of clay puddle which had been heaped against the bank on the valley side to prevent any tendency for the water to percolate through and so undermine it. The reason for this precaution was that a few years previously a sensational burst had occurred at a point known as Sun Bank where the Ruabon–Llangollen railway runs directly below. During the night a substantial portion of the canal bank had given way to produce a cascade of such force and volume that both tracks of the line were undermined, causing the derailment of the unsuspecting early morning 'local'.

I judged that these heaps of puddle had so reduced the width of the channel as to make this part of the canal impassable for a flat-bottomed boat drawing 2 feet, and only navigable by a small cruiser. And even if we did succeed in struggling up to Llangollen, the 'winding' place just beyond the wharf there looked far too choked with the mud of years to enable a 70-foot narrow boat to swing. The prospect of having to stern-haul *Cressy* for the four miles back to the aqueduct was not attractive; so, having accomplished our main objective we decided to call it a day. At the end of the aqueduct we manoeuvred *Cressy* until her stern was under the bridge over the mouth of the Llangollen canal. Then, while Angela and Gunde guided her with shafts, Hugh and I stern-hauled her up the canal for about 200 yards before we moored her up. Thanks to our temporary crew, we now had her pointing in the right direction when the time came to depart; also, the big windows of our sitting cabin looked straight out over the valley and so acute was the bend in the canal that this view included in the middle distance the aqueduct we had so lately crossed. On the opposite side of us and astern was a park-like landscape of heavy trees and greensward. A screen of trees and a steep bank sheltered us from the north and between them and the canal bank was a narrow strip of turf. A more perfect mooring it would be difficult to imagine.

There was one very curious feature of this mooring which may still be seen and which I leave to some enterprising local industrial archaeologist to unravel. This was a single enormous lump of what was undoubtedly tap-cinder from a blast furnace. This stood between our mooring and the bank; at least four feet in diameter, it looked like a strange meteorite, detached as it was from any other vestige of industrial activity. The iron trough of Pont Cysyllte is said to have been cast by Telford's friend William Hazeldine at Plas Kynaston – on a site now built over by the Monsanto Chemical Works – and conveyed by inclined tramway to the aqueduct. But the discovery of this enormous clinker made me wonder whether Hazeldine may have erected a special temporary furnace near the site from which to cast the trough sections. If this was the case, I felt that something must have gone terribly wrong with this operation in order to produce a single mass of clinker of such proportions.

We stayed at this mooring for the best part of three months of perfect summer weather, during which time we entertained on board both old friends who came to stay and new friends whom we made locally. Among the latter was Dorothy Hartley, an elderly spinster who lived with a friend in a cottage at the Vron. The couple reminded us of latter-day Ladies of Llangollen. They had not spotted us when we passed through the Vron, but their curiosity had been aroused by the strange bright blue and scarlet object on the opposite side of the valley so Dorothy Hartley had walked across the aqueduct to investigate, and introduced herself, somewhat diffidently, from the towing path opposite. I am usually embarrassingly bad at connecting names with faces or authors with the right books, but on this occasion the memory bank worked perfectly and I replied as I should: 'Not the author of *Made in England!*' She was visibly delighted to be recognized in this way, displaying a humility which I thought as disarming as it was unjustified, because *Made in England* was perhaps the best book which has ever been written about the English country crafts. Lavishly illustrated by the author's own drawings and photographs, its descriptions are strictly practical and workmanlike and it is refreshingly free from nostalgia and either artfulness or craftyness. It was first published in 1939 and so, like other good books of the period, was swept into oblivion by the war. Already the statement in her preface that the book recorded only living crafts had become almost impossible to believe.

During our stay at Pont Cysyllte, Dorothy Hartley could not have been kinder. Whenever we were away she became *Cressy*'s self-appointed guardian, crossing the aqueduct twice a day to ensure that all was well. She also insisted on pressing upon us the products of her cottage garden and kitchen – and delicious they were for, as one would expect of such an author, she practised what she preached and was highly skilled both as a gardener and as a cook. Needless to say we had a great deal in common and were both sad when the time came for us to sail away. We did not meet again. *Cressy*, too, soon met an old friend. She had not been at her new mooring many hours before a Welsh voice hailed her from the towpath opposite. It turned out to be an elderly local man who had helped to build her in dry dock only a few hundred yards away during the First World War. Truly she had come home.

When we grumble now at the appalling weather of the so-called English summer, it seems that in past summers the sun was always shining. This is partly because, by a kindly dispensation, it is only pleasant features that tend to linger in memory; the grey and sodden days are mercifully forgotten. Partly, though by no means wholly, true, for it is an indisputable fact that the summers during the decade of the sixties were consistently cold, wet and cheerless compared with those we enjoyed during these years on *Cressy*. This statement does not depend on fallible memory but is endorsed by my log in which I made a note of the weather each day. I realize now that this was not because I fancied myself some sea captain in the days of sail to whom the state of the weather was all important and could mean life or death, but simply because, living on a boat, we were far more acutely conscious of, and responsive to, the weather and to our natural environment generally than are those who today spend most of their existence in centrally heated houses, offices or factories, or in heated capsules in transit between them. Not that we led a life of spartan hardship. In times of rough weather we could batten ourselves down snugly enough; it was just that at such times one was ever reminded of the world outside by the sound of the rain pattering on the deck above or by the gentle rocking and nudging of our boat under the buffets of the wind that rattled our windows.

Under such conditions, grey days of ceaseless rain could be extremely depressing; but to such a degree have we now alienated ourselves from the natural world, that few can appreciate that great lifting of the spirits, that mood of exaltation which we experienced when at last the grey clouds dispersed and the sun burst out upon a fresh and glistening world. Our ancestors down to the nineteenth century were similarly deeply affected by the elemental realities of weather and season simply because they lacked the technology that enables us so effectually to insulate ourselves from their effects, greatly to our material comfort but at immeasurable spiritual loss. The still beauty of autumn evenings no longer speaks sadly to us of the mutability of all living things; the freshness of a fine spring morning no longer holds for us the promise of perpetual renewal and rebirth. Just as primitive man celebrated the passing seasons with appropriate ritual, so most great prose and poetry of the past reflects an elemental influence more self-conscious and sophisticated but no less profound.*

My log fully substantiates my recollection that both our pioneering voyages up the Welsh Canal were blessed by unusually perfect summer weather, and I have now attempted to explain how deeply we were able to appreciate it. We were lucky that on both occasions it continued unbroken into September, for August is generally a wet month, particularly in the Welsh mountains. But now there was none of that oppressive atmosphere that had marked the fateful summer when *Cressy* had first sailed out from Banbury ten years before. In 1947 the dry weather had been one factor responsible for an alarming water shortage, but now that the works at Llantisilio had been completed we no longer had any fears on this score. In the narrow channel beside our boat the water flowed past swiftly, deep and crystal, for its seven-mile course along the mountain sides from the Horseshoe Falls had left it quite unpolluted and during the hot days we bathed frequently. By this time we had, I regret to say, substituted an ex-R.A.F. rubber dinghy for Harry Rogers's coracle. Although the ash frame and tarred

---

* One of the very few modern writers to appreciate this is Winifred Gérin. See her *The Effects of Environment on the Brontë Writings*, a lecture read before the Royal Society of Literature in February 1969.

canvas of a Severn coracle was much more appropriate to
Cressy's hull of tarred oak planking, it was far too vulnerable
in the only place where it could be conveniently carried – on
our cabin top, where it was liable to be crushed like an egg-shell
by the first arched bridge. Practically, the rubber dinghy was a
far better substitute because it could so readily be deflated and
stowed. In this craft it took only a few minutes to paddle down
from *Cressy*'s mooring and on to the aqueduct and this became
a popular experience for our visitors, always provided they had
a good head for heights. For if, on looking down from the
highest part, the swiftly moving waters of the Dee below
suddenly appeared to stand still and, instead, the aqueduct
seemed to be toppling, then it was high time that the visitor
was back on terra firma.

I remember one warm and still summer night of such beauty
that, reluctant to close our cabin doors and go to bed, I decided
on a sudden impulse to take this rubber dinghy and paddle it
alone on to the great aqueduct. When I reached the middle I
shipped my paddle and sat quietly, one hand keeping the dinghy
motionless by grasping the edge of the iron trough. It was after
midnight and few lights pricked the darkness of the valley
slopes, but a great golden harvest moon, looking almost as
large and colourful as those we see in Samuel Palmer's visionary and paradisal landscapes, hung low in the sky over the rim
of the southern slopes. There was not a breath of wind and the
only sound was the soothing and ceaseless whispering and
chuckling of the river as it rippled over its boulder-strewn bed
far below. Of all the experiences of that summer, I think this
was the most memorable, although I find it hard to explain
now why this was so. As in an earlier chapter I attempted
inadequately to express the essence of a similar experience at
Llanthony, I will make no second attempt but will only remark
upon certain similarities in the circumstances and surroundings
that evoked them. I think it significant that both should occur
at a late hour on a still and moonlit night. I believe it was no
accident that so many of the pictures Palmer painted during his
great but all too brief visionary period at Shoreham depict the
tranquillity of such a still and silent hour as though he were,

as he said, 'preparing a rest for the people of God'.* The poems of the Silurist, Henry Vaughan, are also, to me, reminiscent of moonlight stillness as I wrote in a book I shall have occasion to mention later.† But for me there had to be another essential ingredient in the scene in order to make possible a brief escape from the temporal into an eternal world (for such I take these experiences to be). This was the presence of a significant work of man's hands. At Llanthony it had been the nave arcades of a ruined priory church which I had surveyed from the height of one of its western towers. Like the great cathedrals, those arches were the masterwork of humble men who recognized, but had not yet learned to bend to their purpose, the wonders of the natural world and believed there was no greater purpose in life than to build to the glory of their supreme author. Now I was again looking down at a dark valley from a lofty vantage, but this time afloat in the air high above it, buoyed up by Thomas Telford's towering stone piers and cradled in iron that had once bubbled white hot in 'Merlin' Hazeldine's furnaces at Plas Kynaston. At the time of its completion, Pont Cysyllte was unique, the grandest embodiment of man's new confidence in his ability to master his environment, of man's faith in his own, rather than in any external, powers. Directly beneath me, fixed to the base of the pier on the southern bank of the river, is a cast-iron plaque bearing a long and flowery inscription celebrating the opening of the aqueduct on 26 November 1805. Much more appropriate, I felt, would be a single brief quotation from a poem by Yeats:

Measurement began our Might.

Maybe it will one day be clear to us that it also began our downfall.

Hugh and Gunde had arrived in the little two-seater open M.G. which he then owned, and although it was a nice little car it

* Quoted by W. B. Yeats in his last valedictory poem.
† *The Clouded Mirror*, Bodley Head, 1955. 'The white radiance of Vaughan's greatest poems is of a quality no longer of this world. One thinks of moonlight reflected in some cold, clear pool not flawed by any stir and fret of wind or current, and for such unearthly tranquillity his poetry is the natural medium.'

was somewhat unsociable. Fortunately, however, my father's sports four-seater Alvis was acting as *Cressy*'s 'land tender' at Pont Cysyllte. I had brought the car into commission for the first time since before the war because my own Alvis was undergoing a protracted engine overhaul at Banbury. In this larger car the four of us were able to make a number of expeditions together through the little mountain roads in the vicinity of the valleys of the Dee, the Ceiriog and the Rhaiadr, the latter with its magnificent waterfall. In perfect summer weather such as we were enjoying there can be no pleasanter vehicle than an open vintage touring car. Cars of this era really are full four-seaters in that they provide ample room for four people to sit in comfort and stretch their legs. Also, because one sits higher than in a modern vehicle, one can fully appreciate all the sights, scents and sounds of summer. It adds up to an almost forgotten form of transport.

As the guests of the Griffiths, we also motored farther afield to the Lleyn Peninsula where we visited Bardsey Island, 'the island of the saints'. After experiencing the passage through Bardsey Sound I can appreciate why, in the Middle Ages, two pilgrimages to Bardsey were worth one to faraway Rome, for it would be difficult to find a trickier piece of water anywhere round the coast of the British Isles. On the day we crossed, a heavy swell was heaving with hollow thunder against the inhospitable rock shelves that wall its shores. Yet, out in the sound, there were circular patches which looked from a distance to be perfectly calm and smooth water. This appearance was wickedly deceptive for, in fact, they were whirlpools or tide rips caused by converging tidal currents, and when we approached them more nearly we could see that they seethed like water in a saucepan just before it boils. The two elderly Welsh fishermen whom we had persuaded to ferry us over from Aberdaron obviously had infinite faith – certainly much more than I possessed – in the mechanical marvels of the modern world. Their open boat was equipped with neither oars nor sail, and they relied entirely on the efforts of an ancient and extremely rusty two-cylinder 'Handy Billy' Thornycroft engine. The two sparking plugs looked as though they were as old as the engine and had never been removed in its lifetime. No wonder the engine sometimes suffered from hiccups. Yet the two old men puffed imperturbably at their foul-smelling pipes as we chuffed slowly through the turbulent waters of the sound, an occasional seal popping a curious head out of the water in our wake to gaze after us with large, dark, wondering eyes. What action would have followed if that engine had suddenly expired it was impossible to imagine, and I did my best to dismiss such speculations from my mind. Our two elderly navigators had obviously done so years before and had so far survived successfully. They knew these treacherous waters like the backs of their hands, for on the return voyage we did not pass again through that alarming sound but, because they judged that wind and tide were unfavourable, went eastabout from the island landing place so that we had circumnavigated Bardsey by the time we landed at Aberdaron in the evening. On the island itself, thanks to Hugh's Anglesey Welsh (the purest Welsh spoken in the Principality, he insisted), the natives were certainly friendly, and if we had been shipwrecked mariners they could not have been kinder or more hospitable. The wife of an island farmer insisted on taking us to her kitchen where she gave us an unforgettable tea of crisp-crusted freshly baked bread and delicious butter of her own churning. I fear that farmhouse may be standing empty and ruinous by now. Even then, I remember, our hostess was worried by the fact that the island children had lately lost their school teacher, and a replacement had not so far been found. Like all island communities, although geographically so near the mainland, Bardsey is isolated by its dangerous seas, sometimes for weeks on end; the problem of providing educational and health services often becomes insuperable, and eventually brings about a sad exodus and desertion.

There is a lighthouse on Bardsey. It stands on the fist of an out-thrusting headland that has nearly become an island, for the sea's rage has almost bitten away the forearm connecting it to the mainland. It consists of a causeway of green turf which, from memory, is not more than ten yards wide at its narrowest point. While the others lay in the sun, I strolled off to look at the lighthouse, and Gunde's little corgi bitch came scampering after me. We had reached the midpoint of the isthmus when

the dog suddenly stopped dead in her tracks; all her hackles
went up and she began a low, continuous growling such as I
had never heard before. I tried to coax her on, but she remained
motionless; it was obvious from her eyes that she feared something which no human eye could see. So I went forward alone
while she scuttled back to her mistress with such little tail as
she had between her legs. This episode convinced me that even
if Bardsey is deserted by human kind, the island will not be
tenantless.

It would be misleading to give an impression that this
summer in Wales was one long golden afternoon of leisure
and pleasure. There was work to be done. I had to spend hours
at my desk on the boat, some of it lucratively and some unpro-
fitably on correspondence concerned with my Hon. Secretaryship of the I.W.A. And while Hugh Griffith was staying with
us he spent much time lying on one of the bunks in our fore-
cabin or outside in the sun studying the part of King Lear
which he had undertaken to play in a production at Swansea
that autumn as part of an Arts Festival. Hugh had convinced
himself, and easily convinced me, that since Lear was an ancient
British king and therefore Celtic, there was no occasion, in
playing him, to disguise his own Welshness. On the contrary,
he had decided that it could be turned to advantage. For
example, in the famous scene on the heath when Lear at once
invokes and defies the storm in the speech beginning: 'Blow,
winds, and crack your cheeks! rage! blow!', he proposed to use
the Welsh *hwyl*, an indescribable kind of incantatory intonation
that was used by certain Welsh preachers when they felt themselves inspired with the gift of tongues. This interpretation of
the part and the manner of its playing – determined so appro-
priately almost within the shadow of the hill-top castle of Dinas
Bran that could have been the ruins of Lear's palace – certainly
worked. We made the long journey to Swansea that autumn
specially to see the result, and were rewarded by a memorable
theatrical experience. It was certainly the finest and the most
moving performance of the proud, distracted King that I have
ever seen, either before or since. In playing Lear, even the
finest English actors appear too intellectual and civilized to my
way of thinking. They cannot bring to the part that mysterious

quality, 'fire in the belly', which only the Celtic people, certainly among northern races, appear to possess.

At last a glorious summer drew to an end and it was time to be gone. *Cressy's* engine throbbed again after long idleness; sadly we took in and coiled our mooring lines. After so much sunshine, the weather was still fine but now overcast, and although it was quite windless there was a first chill breath of autumn in the air as we passed once more on to the great aqueduct and headed southwards. Our destination was Gayton 'Arm End', near Northampton. It will be remembered that we had lain at Gayton temporarily after our first voyage to the Welsh Canal, but this time we decided to desert Banbury for once and make Gayton our winter quarters.

Chapter 8

The End of the Cut

Something about the Welsh Canal seemed to foster ideas so far as I was concerned. On our first visit there I had conceived a Canal Exhibition in London and now, on this second occasion, the thought suddenly struck me – why not organize a rally of boats? I had in mind a kind of aquatic version of the Vintage Sports Car Club's Rally to Presteigne which I had first helped to organize just before the war and which had proved so popular that it had since become an annual event. In the Presteigne Rally we had an award for the car coming the greatest distance, competitors sending telegrams from various towns en route as proof that they had been there. A prize was also awarded for the best maintained car and so on. It seemed to me that precisely the same sort of system could be applied to the inland water-ways. It would be fun for the competitors and at the same time be an object lesson to the lay public, who were at that time woefully ignorant on the subject. It would show them what improbably lengthy journeys could be made by using the canals and rivers of England.

This idea of a rally of boats having germinated, the next question to be decided was where to hold it, and here the range of choice was naturally much more limited than in the case of the vintage car rally where the choice of Presteigne, popular though it proved, was purely fortuitous. There were a number of conditions that the site had to meet. Because there was then considerable commercial traffic over most of the system, the rally would have to be held somewhere off the main routes where such an assemblage of boats would not cause an obstruc-

166

tion. Also, the site should not be on the narrow canal system where it would be inaccessible by broad-beamed river craft, a fact which, in these early days, would mean a seriously restricted entry. Finally, I felt that I should seek a place somewhere in central England, equally accessible from the four quarters of the compass. Pondering this, I looked hard and long at the large map of the canal system which almost covered one wall panel of *Cressy*'s sitting cabin. This map had originally been published by the old Grand Union Canal Company, and, although it marked all the inland waterways, the G.U.C. system was shown as a heavy blue line extending from London to Birmingham with a long secondary main line thrusting up into the east Midlands through Leicester and Loughborough to terminate at Langley Mill, near Nottingham. These primary routes threw off branches to Slough, to Aylesbury, to North-ampton and to Market Harborough. I considered the merits of each of these in turn and came down overwhelmingly in favour of the last named.

The branch canal to Market Harborough from the bottom of the locks at Foxton on the 'Leicester Line' is just under six miles long and I was familiar with it because I had made Market Harborough a port of call, as described in *Narrow Boat*, on our first voyage just before the war. It was then still occa-sionally used by boats carrying imported soft wood from Brentford which was off-loaded at a timber yard beside the capacious basin at Market Harborough. But it had since become completely disused although, when we had last passed that way in 1947, travelling south from the Welsh Canal towards Gayton, it had still looked readily navigable apart from a cer-tain amount of weed on the surface – and there were no locks on the branch to fall into disrepair. In fact, in origin it was not a branch at all, but part of the Leicester & Northamptonshire Union Canal, an abortive project for a broad canal which was intended to link the river Soar at Leicester with the Nene at Northampton but expired at Market Harborough when the money ran out. It was the later construction of the original Grand Union Canal from Norton Junction to Foxton that finally supplied the missing link between the east Midlands and the south, but only by narrow canal. However, it would be possible for wide-beam boats to reach Market Harborough from the river Trent and its associated waterways.

It was thus settled that the Association's first rally of boats should be organized at Market Harborough in the following summer and this was one reason why we chose Gayton instead of Banbury as a winter mooring; so far as the organization of the event was concerned it was strategically placed about half-way between Market Harborough and London. There was another good reason why we had chosen Gayton. I had just been commissioned by Harry Batsford to write a book about the Thames to accompany a set of engravings, paintings and colour prints which he had collected. I had accepted this invitation with alacrity because I saw in it a means of achieving another ambition, which was to navigate the whole course of the non-tidal Thames. My only previous experience of the river had been our two wartime journeys between Oxford and Reading, when the Conservancy had waived the licence fee because I was only using the river 'in the course of a through journey between one waterway and another'. But now that the Thames & Severn Canal had long lain derelict, there could be no such excuse for navigating the river up to Lechlade, and for a craft of maximum size – which was what *Cressy* was in the eyes of the Conservators – the cost of an annual licence, plus the total dues on forty-six locks, added up to much more than my shallow pocket could afford. But now, because I was writing a book on their river, the Conservators had very generously waived their charges and presented *Cressy* with a free licence plate and myself with a free lock pass. So, as soon as the spring came, we planned to sail straight down the main line of the Grand Union Canal towards London and enter the Thames at Brentford.

It must have been some time in October or early November that Robert Aickman, myself and our respective wives paid a joint visit to Market Harborough to look at the suitability of the canal there and to broach the project to the Town Council who swallowed the idea enthusiastically and, in the event, cooperated splendidly. This was the last occasion on which the first Chairman and the first Honorary Secretary of the Inland Waterways Association cooperated together, for it was not long before I wrote in to the I.W.A. office in Gower Street and tendered my resignation.

This was not a step I had lightly taken as a result of some passing mood of pique or exasperation, but the result of a difficult decision which I had only reached after much careful thought and long discussion with Angela. It was made for a variety of reasons, one of which was quite simply that I could not afford to continue. The success of my 'design for living' depended on my earning my living by writing, and the cold fact was that since I had cheerfully thrown up my wartime job and resumed my original pre-war plan I had not been paying my way. Indeed, without Angela's slender allowance (which was never assured anyway) we should have been on the financial rocks already. As a result of the success of my first book, I had allowed myself to become involved in a canal campaign which entailed far more unpaid work than I could properly afford. I reflected that if I had had to hold down a job over the three and a half years that had passed since the I.W.A. had been launched, I would have been quite unable to undertake the amount of active campaigning which I had done. I was discovering that a free-lance is always under pressure from others who assume that his time is his own, and it requires great self-discipline to resist such blandishments. He can easily find himself caught up in a plethora of unrewarding – and often thankless – 'honorary' tasks. Added to this was the fact that we both realized I was forfeiting the freedom which I had gone to the canals to seek. As the Association grew rapidly in stature and influence, this had become the more apparent. We no longer felt ourselves to be free agents; *Cressy* and her crew had become, by almost imperceptible degrees, the tool of the Gower Street office. Angela had been the first to realize this, and had been urging me for some time to be quit of the Association. I was less perceptive, and was also keener perhaps that a crusade to which I had set my hands should succeed. For this reason I tended to turn a blind eye to what was happening or pretend that it did not exist. The brutal truth was now becoming only too clear, it was becoming a band-wagon, as good causes, often started with the best of intentions, are apt to do, such being the frailty of human nature. We, who had originally sought refuge on the canals to escape from all we disliked in the modern world, deeply resented what we felt to be our exploitation for such purposes by others. The moment of truth so far as I was concerned occurred one morning at Gayton when there arrived a letter telling me to attend a meeting at Newbury in three days' time, couched in terms which I would have hesitated to use to anyone. Needless to add, I did not go.

Two other considerations played their part in a decision which was destined to have far-reaching consequences. One was the knowledge that the Association was by now so firmly established that it was certainly strong enough to survive the loss of any single individual connected with it, be he never so active in its affairs. The other was that I found myself increasingly out of sympathy with the Association's declared aim to restore to navigable order 'every navigable waterway'. With our limited resources of money and manpower this aim, it seemed to me, had inevitably led to too great a concentration of effort upon reviving the dead branches of a shrinking system at the expense of those parts of the tree which were still more or less precariously alive. What chiefly appealed to me about the canal system was its indigenous working life. On the narrow canals this meant the working narrow boats and their crews which were so essential a part of them. These working boaters, so many of whom I knew and admired, unconsciously supplied that subtle traditional patina of constant use – the worn and dusty towpath, the polish that generations of 'uphill or downhill straps' had given to the, bollards of cast-iron or grainy oak at the locks; it was an essential part of that blend of utility and beauty which used to compound the particular magic of canals. This was something which some members in the I.W.A. could never fully appreciate. They could value canals aesthetically as an important contribution to landscape beauty, but they could not assess to how great an extent utility was responsible for this. In just the same way, urban man can never appreciate to what extent the changing methods of agriculture affect the beauty of the rural landscape. For this reason I felt we had been devoting far too great a proportion of our effort to the 'fringe' waterways at the expense of canals such as the Trent & Mersey or the southern part of the Oxford

Canal which were still alive. On these latter canals and on many others, trade still persisted stubbornly in the face of manifold discouragements. The captain of a pair of working narrow boats was paid for each particular trip at a rate of so much per ton carried. Considering that such payments covered the unpaid labour of his wife and family, as well as that of the captain himself, they amounted to little more than a starvation wage. For this inadequate return there were a number of reasons: the undredged state of the canals which both slowed the boats down and prevented them loading to their full capacity; the lack of any serious coordinated attempt to obtain back-loads which meant that boat captains spent far too high a proportion of their time travelling light for which they were paid only a low flat rate. Again, no attempt had been made over the years to reduce turn-round time by improving methods of loading and, particularly, of discharging boats. How often had I watched men take all day to unload twenty-five tons of coal from a narrow boat at Banbury Wharf using shovels and barrows, and reflected that the use of even the simplest form of mechanical elevator would have saved a great deal of back-breaking toil and reduced turn-round time by at least a half. Finally, the future of the family boat was also seriously threatened at this time, as it had been in the past, by reformers who would take the children off the boats, thus destroying the traditional family life of the boaters in the name of the sacred cow of education.

During these first years of the Association, I and a small minority who shared my point of view, such as those women who had served on the canals during the war and so become acquainted with the life of the canals, did what we could to campaign for more favourable conditions for the boaters. It has since become obvious that, if one accepts modern economic doctrines, the canal narrow boat was doomed to extinction by its small pay-load. Nevertheless, had all the reforms and improvements we pressed for in 1948–9 been carried out, I sincerely believe that the life of the working narrow boat might have been prolonged by at least ten years. One of the reforms we advocated was that the antiquated and complex system of toll charges based on tonnage should be swept away and replaced by a simple system of annual licence fees per boat. This sensible suggestion was ultimately adopted, but only many years later, by which time traffic on the narrow canal system had dwindled almost to vanishing point and no such transfusion could revivify the dying patient.

Although our campaign to ease the lot of the working boatmen received token support from some members, it never attracted the amount of publicity, attention and time that was devoted, for example, to the Kennet & Avon. This canal was of singular beauty and character as I knew very well, being the only person in the I.W.A. who at that time had actually navigated it. But since I had done so in 1940 the K. & A. had become virtually derelict, and the prospect of reviving commercial traffic on it was extremely remote. I was by no means guiltless in this matter myself because, largely for sentimental reasons of my own, I had devoted too much time to the Welsh Canal, another waterway whose commercial prospects were practically nil. It was because, I now think, of this failure to get our priorities right at the outset that the Association suddenly awoke to the unpleasant fact that traffic over the whole system of narrow waterways had ceased, and that as a result, canals which had hitherto received scant attention were suddenly at risk.

So, for all these associated reasons I dispatched my letter of resignation to Gower Street. I explained that the post of Honorary Secretary had become too onerous but that I hoped to remain as an ordinary member of the committee and would continue to help the Association in any way that I could. It is difficult to credit the almost hysterical reaction aroused by my resignation. It had been a case of 'united we stand, divided we fall', and by my sudden defection I had dealt the cause a traitorous and near fatal blow. If I persisted in my folly I could expect no further toleration. I was momentarily winded by this response as though someone had hit me in the solar plexus. No one could care more about the canals than I did, but this struck me as pitching things too high. It was as though I had committed heresy and high treason at one and the same time, and from that day forward *Cressy* and her crew found themselves increasingly ostracized by part of the membership.

We were both members of the committee responsible for organizing the Market Harborough Rally, until we learned that some members of that committee were organizing a play during the rally in which they had the leading roles. I felt it was their job to organize a rally rather than spend time on a venture which I thought was of no conceivable use or relevance so far as the waterways were concerned. For expressing this point of view, Angela and I were both made to feel that our continuing presence on the rally committee could not be tolerated.

Had my resignation not provoked so violent and hostile a reaction, the whole affair might have passed over peacefully enough; but as it was, it developed into a major row which split the Association from top to bottom. Our position inevitably attracted sympathizers, with the result that I found myself landed willy-nilly at the centre of a very vocal 'splinter group' claiming to champion the cause of the working boatmen and, quite as importantly, advocating a more democratic I.W.A. As happens in politics when similar situations develop, one side or the other sooner or later resorts to unfortunate tactics whereupon, human nature being what it is, the other side retaliates in kind so that the outsider can be forgiven for saying 'a plague on both your houses'. So it was in this case. Although I can now see it merely as a storm in a teacup, it then seemed a serious affair.

One small but humorous episode is sufficient to reveal the tenor of events in the canal world during 1950. When I had first launched my proposal for a rally of boats at Market Harborough, I had suggested that cups should be presented to the winning boats as was customary at the vintage car rally at Presteigne. This idea was accepted; it was proposed that each member of the committee should present a cup for a specific object (mine, I remember, was for the best kept engine-room) and we all trooped along to the Silver Vaults to select our respective trophies having agreed to pool the expense between us, leaving it to the Gower Street office to arrange for the engraving. Because we hoped that the rally would become an annual event, we all assumed that these would become perpetual challenge trophies to be competed for each year, the winner being awarded a small replica as is usual in events of this kind. Not until the rally programme appeared did we discover to our astonishment that we were most generously giving away our costly trophies and that only one of them was perpetual.

In the light of the strained situation it was a great relief when a long winter came to an end and we could be under way again, heading south down the Grand Union Canal. It was over ten years (1938) since I had last taken *Cressy* over this part of the canal, and then it had only been as far as Watford. Now we were to follow it to its end – or beginning – at Brentford. We locked down through the entrance locks at Brentford with the incoming tide, choosing our moment to slip out into the broad tideway of London River before the tugs, towing their barges high laden with esparto grass bound for the paper mills of Apsley and Croxley, arrived off the entrance. This one-and-only excursion into tidal waters was very brief indeed. Borne swiftly upstream by the last of the flood, *Cressy* swept through the open half-tidal lock at Richmond and was soon approaching Teddington Lock, the first under the jurisdiction of the Thames Conservancy and the entrance to the non-tidal Thames.

Although it has long been out of print, I have described *Cressy*'s Thames journey from Teddington to Lechlade so fully in *The Thames from Mouth to Source* that I will not do so again. The more perceptive readers of that book may notice that there is a certain sad, elegiac quality about the writing in some places. As *Cressy* made her slow way westwards up the great river in the golden weather of early June, I think I secretly knew in my heart of hearts that, so far as our design for living was concerned, this was to be the last summer.

There could be no greater contrast than that between the two largest of English rivers, Severn and Thames. Although the greater part of Severn's course is in England and it flows through the capital cities of three English shires, to call it an English river seems a misnomer because it retains to a remarkable degree the quality of the land of its birth. It is essentially a Celtic river of a character that has never been tamed. By contrast, the Thames seemed as thoroughly domesticated and placid as a lake created by Capability Brown in some nobleman's park. Whereas it was not until the 40s and 50s of last century that Severn's primitive violence was partially tamed in its lower reaches by the construction of the present infrequent locks, Thames has been domesticated by man for centuries past and its many locks are the successors of ancient flash locks whose origins go back to the Middle Ages. Consequently Thames seems to have long forgotten its native wildness, and the reaches between the locks appeared to us to resemble a string of lakes rather than a great river. Even its floods lack the headstrong violence of the swift Severn spates, Thames waters rising with slow and silent stealth to creep almost apologetically round the willow boles and out over the wide water-meadows.

The part of the river that we liked the best is also sometimes called the Isis, in other words it consists of the upper reaches west of Oxford. It was, and maybe still is, less frequented than that below Oxford, because Osney Bridge with its restricted headway excludes the large Thames cruisers. This upper river was the last to be improved by the substitution of pound locks for the ancient navigation weirs. From Medley to Godstow Lock beside Port Meadow is the last of the broad, lake-like reaches. Once through Godstow we found ourselves in a river of much smaller scale and more natural and unpretentious character than the lower Thames, a river that reminded us of the Warwickshire Avon above Tewkesbury except that its broad valley lacked the bold focal point of Bredon Hill. Instead, upon our left hand across a wide expanse of willow-bordered water-meadows, there was only the misty blue outline of that long, undulating ridge of high ground that stretches from the wooded Cumnor Hills by Oxford into Wiltshire through Faringdon and Highworth. In 1950, this upper river seemed lost and almost incredibly remote considering the populous countryside through which it passes. Whereas the lower reaches had been busy with every sort of pleasure craft from punts and skiffs at one end of the scale to Salters' steamers at the other, I cannot recall that we passed a single boat on the move between Oxford and Lechlade. Perhaps this was just as well because, particularly in its uppermost reaches, the river becomes so narrow and tortuous that it was only with difficulty that I was able to swing *Cressy*'s seventy-foot length through the bends and, in the process, took up the whole width of the channel; for any craft approaching downstream a collision would have been almost impossible to avoid.

Having reached our journey's end, we winded *Cressy* just above the single stone arch of Halfpenny bridge at Lechlade before tying up in the shade of the willows at the foot of the town meadow below the bridge. It was early June, roses were everywhere blooming in profusion against walls of grey stone and the hay had not yet been cut. It was also the first occasion that we had tied up in Gloucestershire since we had moored at Sharpness two years before.

From bills posted in the square of the little town we learned that on the morrow John Betjeman was to open a village fête in the grounds of Buscot Rectory. I determined to go and, if possible, make his acquaintance. The fact that I had long admired his poetry was not, in itself, a sufficiently good reason for such a resolve. Because writers and artists put the best of themselves into their work, it necessarily follows that they cannot themselves be better than their work and indeed often appear distinctly inferior. In fact, with rare exceptions, the greater the art the lesser its creator appears by comparison. It is for this very simple and obvious reason that 'fans' are all doomed to disillusion. They expect to find a soul-mate or a super human being and instead find themselves in an embarrassing confrontation with a very ordinary individual who looks abstracted if not positively distracted as he mumbles some platitude or scratches his ear with a glazed look in his eye. Yet it was not as a fan but for a purely practical reason that I was anxious to meet John Betjeman.

One of the most looked-forward-to objectives of this voyage was a visit to Kelmscott Manor. My admiration for William Morris had made this house which he had loved an object of pilgrimage, and I felt that my book about the Thames would be incomplete if I failed to record in it my impressions of Kelmscott. Behind a screen of sheltering elms, we had caught a brief glimpse of its stone chimneys and gables as *Cressy* swung round the bends beyond Eaton Hastings; but when we reached Lechlade we discovered to our dismay that the Manor was locked and empty, the tenants who leased it from its Oxford Collegiate owners having recently departed. This was a great disappointment, but our spirits rose when we learned that John Betjeman had taken up the lease of Kelmscott, not because he had any intention of living there but from the purely altruistic motive of safeguarding it. For, incredible though it may now seem, the future of Kelmscott was at that time in some doubt.

We walked over St John's bridge to Buscot to find the usual tables piled with cast-off clothing and Women's Institute jams, the bran tub and the bowling-for-the-pig, laid out on the rectory lawn. John Betjeman had obviously been lunching with the rector for, accompanied by his host, he eventually appeared in the doorway of the Georgian house. I remember thinking that, in his straw boater and suit of clerical grey, he looked much more like the popular image of a country parson than the rector himself. Soon we got into conversation and I was gratified to discover that my name as a writer was not unknown to him. He at once linked my name with my book about the Irish canals, *Green and Silver*, which had been published the previous year, and this pleased me particularly. *Narrow Boat* had proved almost too successful. I had grown sick of being greeted or introduced as 'the man who wrote *Narrow Boat*'.

As for visiting Kelmscott, that was easily arranged. The next evening we were hailed from the water and looked out of *Cressy*'s windows to see John Betjeman punting Osbert Lancaster downstream towards us. As both were wearing straw boaters, they might have punted straight out of Edwardian England. If we cared to meet John at Kelmscott on the following afternoon, he would open the house up for us. I duly recorded my impressions of that visit in my book and, reading them again at this distance of time, I feel sure that if I were to revisit Kelmscott today my reactions would be very different. With youthful arrogance, I then considered both the Pre-Raphaelite and the Art and Craft movements, between which Morris was the linking figure, to be totally inadequate kicks against the pricks of the new industrial machine society which had already come to birth. I dismissed too arbitrarily, as ephemeral and self-conscious, the relics of Morris and Rossetti's occupation of Kelmscott, compared with the timeless tradition of Cotswold building which the house itself exemplified. But it must be remembered that Kelmscott was then standing empty following a long occupation by tenants who, it was obvious, had not been over-conscientious. This gave to the whole property a forlorn, neglected air very different, I imagine, from its appearance today. To add a lighter note which I did not touch upon in my Thames book, my attention was struck by an elegant little stone pavilion in one corner of the overgrown garden. This, as John disclosed to us, in fact housed a 'three holer' and he went on to explain how, in gratitude for his action in saving Kelmscott, Osbert Lancaster had recently presented him with a drawing of Janey Morris enthroned on the central seat with Morris and Rossetti on either side.

So idyllic was this mooring at Lechlade, so secluded and yet so conveniently close to the little town, that we seriously considered giving the Market Harborough Rally in August a miss and staying put until the autumn as we had done at Pont Cysyllte the previous year. We were undoubtedly swayed towards such a course by the change in our relations with the I.W.A. which had occurred since I had given up the secretaryship. Then two letters arrived which caused us to change our minds.

The contents of the first letter were so surprising that they made me gasp and stretch my eyes. It was suggested that nothing but harm could result from our bringing *Cressy* to Market Harborough and in strongest terms requested a withdrawal of our entry. Although I felt nothing but contempt for a childish prohibition that could not be enforced, how much pleasanter it would be, I argued, to lie here instead of journeying half across England in order to push *Cressy*'s bows into a hornet's nest. But Angela thought very differently. Her reaction to the letter was much more tigerish and belligerent. The rally had been my idea in the first place and the canals were free for all on payment of tolls, so who the hell presumed to stop *Cressy*?

That I eventually allowed Angela's argument to prevail over my own judgement was due to the contents of the second letter, which came from Philip Unwin of George Allen & Unwin. It was he who had published *Green and Silver*, and this year he was to publish my *Inland Waterways of England*, a purely factual and practical book about the canals and rivers for which I felt there was a need. Publication date for this new book happened to coincide with the rally week, but this was purely coincidental because to use such an occasion as a vehicle for personal publicity had simply never occurred to me and I had left my publishers in ignorance of the rally date. A bewildered Philip Unwin wrote to say that he now understood from the Association that there was strong opposition to any publicity for myself or the book at the rally. This was the last straw. My reaction was not to indulge in lengthy explanations but simply to tell him to ignore the whole episode. For the truth was that such an unwarrantable interference with my private literary affairs at first made me so hopping mad that for the only time in my life I contemplated litigation. Thank goodness I had cooled off and begun to see the absurd side of the whole affair before rushing into an action of uncertain outcome but certain great expense.

Although I soon dropped any idea of litigation, this second letter did make me angry enough to swing round to Angela's point of view, and from that moment it was a case of 'to hell or Market Harborough' where *Cressy* was concerned. These two actions that then seemed so provoking have, with the passage of time, come to appear trivial and even ludicrous. But for this, my publishers would never have heard of Market Harborough, and Philip Unwin would certainly not have visited the rally himself as he did. But for this we might never have left that so pleasant mooring at Lechlade.

The day after leaving Lechlade we were passing through 'the Duke's Cut' on our way to the Oxford Canal. This was a short canal built in 1789 by the Duke of Marlborough to provide a link between the canal and the Wolvercote backwater of the Upper Thames. Until Isis Lock was opened at Oxford in 1796 it was the only connection between canal and river, and, even after Isis was opened, the Duke's Cut continued to be used by boats passing between the Upper Thames and the canal. Considerable narrow boat traffic had used this route within the memory of boaters then still living. James Harwood of *Searchlight*, one of my Oxford Canal boater friends, had told me many a yarn of how he used to work 'up the west country' as a young man, including the frightening way his boat had to be winched up through the old navigation weirs which then still existed on this part of the river. But by 1950 such traffic was no more than a memory and the only commercial craft using the Duke's Cut was an occasional pair of boats carrying a load of coal to Wolvercote Mill. This was a paper mill owned by the Oxford University Press whose speciality was making India paper, famous for the way it combined extreme thinness with opacity. As luck would have it, we encountered our friends the Humphries with their beautiful pair of boats making one of their rare trips to Wolvercote Mill. He was a burly, powerfully built man who it would have been comforting to have on one's side in a rough house. His wife, a striking blonde, wore her hair in coiled plaits about her ears. When we had first got to know them, the family lived on a horse-boat, the *Captain Cook*, but although this was one of the few on the canal that still boasted a fore-cabin, it eventually became totally inadequate for their lengthening string of blond children, so they had graduated to a motor and butty. We met them at the junction of the cut with the backwater where they were performing the complicated manoeuvre of winding both boats and then 'breasting up' (tying up the pair side by side) before dropping astern down the backwater to the mill. They were the first working narrow boats we had seen since we had left Brentford two months before, and it was like coming home to one's native parish. We slowed down and exchanged shouted greetings and news before forging ahead into the narrow, willow-bordered cut that led beneath the railway and so into the Oxford canal where we swung north.

I think this was the only occasion when we passed our familiar moorings at Tooley's Yard, Banbury, without stopping. For we were in a hurry, and felt that by stopping we should all too easily be beguiled by old friends into lingering too long, especially as this had been the first occasion when we had not wintered there. So we lay for the night in the solitude of the disused Twyford Wharf just to the south of the town and slipped unobtrusively through Banbury in the early hours of the following morning. We were at Braunston by nightfall and the next day saw us on the long summit level of 'the Leicester Line' and within striking distance of our objective.

As we approached Market Harborough I was astounded by

the number of boats which had come to the rally. Moored stem to stern, they must have stretched for more than half a mile along the towpath. When I had first conceived the rally I had no idea it would prove so popular; indeed I had not realized that there were so many craft in England capable of navigating the narrow canal system – for it emerged that the majority of the entrants had come from the south through the narrow locks at Watford and Foxton. As *Cressy* drifted slowly past the long line of moored craft we received many a wave and friendly greeting from people we had encountered on earlier voyages, but when we entered the terminal basin we had a very different reception. I had decided to wind *Cressy* in the basin before returning to our mooring so as to be pointing in the right direction when the time came to move off. *Beatrice* was acting as the official headquarters of the rally and so this replica of *Cressy* occupied the most prominent position in the basin. Although we tried to appear totally unconcerned, we were well aware of hostile eyes peering at us through the window curtains. I felt sure that had *Beatrice* been equipped with torpedo tubes, *Cressy* would have gone straight to the bottom. It suddenly seemed very important to put up a bravura performance in the face of this antagonism so we winded *Cressy* without touching a shaft or putting a line ashore but using only rudder and propeller. Alas, this was pride before a fall. A few minutes later, when Angela was standing on our cabin top and bringing *Cressy* broadside into her mooring with our long shaft, the tip of the shaft unexpectedly lost purchase and Angela took a beautiful header into the canal. Fortunately, by this time we were out of sight of the basin and back among friends who could regard such a mishap totally without malice.

The rally was voted a great success, for I suppose only a small minority realized the absurdity of the two rival factions at the centre of things, circling each other warily like predatory tomcats. I think dear old Sir Alan Herbert, the Association's President, realized that there was some breach in the ranks and attempted to mend it by asking if he might visit *Cressy*. It was a most pleasant occasion and we spent a long while drinking and yarning, but I fear it did more harm than good. Things had by now reached such a pass that our opponents could not do other than impute evil intentions to our every action. I think they firmly believed we had inveigled A.P.H. aboard, plied him with liquor and then vilified themselves, whereas it would never have occurred to us to ruin a happy evening by thinking of such things, let alone indulging in deliberate denigration which would assuredly have recoiled upon us.

Although the unpleasant atmosphere clung about *Cressy* like a miasma, so that I could not forget it and often secretly regretted that we had ever left Lechlade, it would be too much to say that we did not enjoy the occasion. The weather was perfect throughout and we thoroughly enjoyed entertaining, and being entertained by, the many old friends we met there. There were working boats at the rally as well as pleasure boats, something that can no longer happen today, more's the pity. A resplendent pair of 'Ovaltine boats'* lay in the basin and won the prize for the best kept pair of working boats. Another pair, the motor *Cairo* and the butty *Warwick* from the Samuel Barlow Coal Company, had benches in their holds and ran regular trips for visitors between the basin and the junction. The Market Harborough Council played their part by arranging a truly splendid display of fireworks to round off the proceedings on the last night.

From Market Harborough we returned by easy stages to our familiar moorings at Banbury for the winter. It was to be the most unhappy winter and early spring of my life. The prime cause of this was that my relationship with Angela had been deteriorating ever since our summer at Pont Cysyllte. I will not attempt to explain why this was. There are some things which a biographer, writing in the future, may nose out if he can, thereby shedding fresh light on his chosen character, but such things are not to be set down in an autobiography. An account of a broken relationship between two people must, if written by one of them even after the passage of years and with the utmost magnanimity, inevitably present a partial view of such a painful event. As I wrote in the first volume of this autobiography, I believe that the extraordinary, implacable hostility of Angela's parents towards her marriage, by cutting

* The firm of A. Wander & Co., the makers of Ovaltine, then owned their own boats to supply their canal-side factory with coal from the Midlands.

themselves off from her for good, placed an intolerable psychological burden upon her which I did not fully appreciate at the
time. Let us leave it at that. Two other factors combined to
complicate and aggravate this domestic crisis. One was the
state of *Cressy* and the other was our deteriorating relations
with the I.W.A.

It is easy to be wise after the event, but a fatal error had been
made when *Cressy* had first been converted into a houseboat
twenty years before. This was a failure to provide through
ventilation under the floorings. These floorings fit flush with,
and on either side of, the oak keelson. This means that there is a
space beneath the floorings and the elm bottoms of the boat
equal to the thickness of the keelson – usually not more than
six inches. On a working narrow boat it was usual to take up
these floorings when the hold was cleaned out after each trip;
but on a houseboat, provision for lifting the floorings is seldom
or never made with the consequence that, unless there is some
special arrangement for through ventilation, the space beneath
becomes an ideal breeding ground for dry and wet rot. In the
case of *Cressy* this was aggravated by the fact that all the rain-
water falling on the little open deck for'ard had to pass through
this under-floor space to collect in the bilges aft where it was
pumped out – the boat being trimmed to be down by the stern
to ensure that the twenty-two-inch propeller was under water.
I had been fighting rot on *Cressy* for years before I realized the
source of the trouble, and now it was too late. Although to an
undiscerning eye she looked as bright and as beautiful as ever,
only I knew that she was like some elephant stricken with a
mortal disease and, as old elephants and old boats do, she had
to find a place to die; to rot away in some old, abandoned
winding hole or wharf, her bare ribs hidden by the kindly
reeds. I had set so much store by my idea of living afloat on the
canals, had pondered it so long before it was finally achieved,
that to bring it to such a sad end was something I could not
contemplate coldly. Over the years I had come to love *Cressy*. It
was an affection that was more than house-pride. I can only
explain it as a combination of love for a home which one has
created oneself with the kind of affection one feels for an old and
trusty vintage car that has carried one staunchly through the

years over countless thousands of miles. Yet an end had now become inevitable. To restore *Cressy* to perfect order would mean virtually a new boat in which nothing would be left of the original but the iron knees. Even if everything else had been right in my life, I could not possibly have afforded such a costly rebuild.

I realized now that I had been so enamoured of my design for living that I had never clearly envisaged what my next step would be when, as all things must, it came to an end. Three factors now combined to make me feel disillusioned with the English canals: the present Association unpleasantness; the visible decline in commercial canal carrying; and, lastly and ironically, the fact that, largely as a result of my own efforts as a publicist, what had been a secret world was now obviously in process of becoming a fashionable playground for frustrated urban man. The question was: what next? On this, Angela and I flatly disagreed.

Curiously enough, although it was I who had suggested our present way of living in the first place, I discovered that her wanderlust was much stronger and more deep-rooted than my own. To Angela the answer to the question seemed obvious – a bigger and better version of *Cressy*, a converted sailing barge of some kind in which we could cross the narrow seas and so explore the continental canal network. I could not see how we could possibly afford such a craft, but in any event I did not relish the idea. I have never been drawn to the sea and the prospect of continental travel, even by canal, did not appeal to me. With all their faults it was the British Isles that had prior claim on my affections, and there was so much of them still to see that I doubted whether even the longest lifetime would allow me time enough.

For this and other reasons it had become clear by Christmas that our life on *Cressy* was fast running out and, as if this alone were not hard enough to bear, that winter was bedevilled by more unpleasantness in the Inland Waterways Association. The immediate cause of this was that the opposing faction put forward a new constitution which rapidly spread alarm and despondency among a small, but extremely active and influential group of long-standing members who constituted themselves an opposition party with R. H. Wyatt of Stone acting as a kind of liaison officer and coordinator.

I remember one dark winter night at Banbury when, like some gunpowder-plot conspirator, Wyatt came to visit me unexpectedly on *Cressy* and we agreed to circulate the whole I.W.A. membership with a statement over our several names. This statement not only called attention to the dangers in the proposed changes in the constitution but it also stressed that the I.W.A. must in future do more to help the working boatmen, including more attention to that part of the narrow canal system which was still in commercial use. Wyatt undertook to duplicate this document and to send it to all members. I still wonder whether I was right to put my name to this statement and so, inevitably, to be regarded by the membership as the spearhead of a dissident movement and, by the opposition, as a deadly rival struggling for power. Under all the circumstances I had never felt less in the mood for a power struggle; on the contrary, I only wished to have done with the whole silly business. But then I reflected that, had it not been for me, most of those who signed this heretical document would never have joined the Association, and so would never have become embroiled in such a squalid affair. For this reason I decided, rightly or wrongly, that I could not let them down and so added my name to theirs. The result of all this was that the date of a special general meeting was fixed in Birmingham in the early spring at which the issue would be finally decided.

This was the spring of 1951 when life on *Cressy* was drawing to its expected end. For the sum of £10 Angela bought herself a 'flat-nose' Morris Oxford two-seater coupé. It both looked and sounded pretty down-at-heel, but after suitable treatment by me it became reasonably reliable. When she had stowed her belongings in the dickey, I watched from *Cressy's* deck as she drove away over the wooden drawbridge at the end of Factory Street. I then went below into a boat that suddenly seemed to have become very silent. Twenty years were to pass before I saw Angela again, and for her they were to be years of wandering, beginning with a long spell of travelling with Billy Smart's circus. As for myself, I soon took *Cressy* away from Tooley's Boatyard and, with the help of a

good friend, Melville Russell-Cooke, worked her northwards
to Stone where R. H. Wyatt had told me he had a customer
eager to buy her. But one cannot leave the past behind as
easily as that; every yard of the canal was haunted by memories
of past voyages. The presence of 'Mel' undoubtedly helped to
make this gloomy last voyage bearable. She had never been on a
canal before, and it was a new and rich experience which she
relished hugely and to which she often referred in later years.
Although no longer in her first youth she scorned my offer of
the sprung berth in the stateroom, electing to sleep on the hard
spare berth in the fore-cabin so that she could be up betimes to
cook the breakfast. For a tyro she was also surprisingly
efficient as a lock-wheeler; her only serious error was to drop
one of my windlasses into a lock chamber. A perfectionist in
everything she undertook, Mel never forgot this incident. At
Great Haywood, she had to leave to catch a train at Stafford
and this meant that I had to journey on alone to Stone Wharf.
The last ten miles and nine locks were into the low sunlight of
a perfect spring evening. To say that I felt sad would be a gross
understatement, and yet it struck me as only fitting that *Cressy*
and I, who had voyaged together through so many years,
should now complete our last journey alone.

When eventually I pulled in to Stone Wharf just as dusk was
falling, Wyatt was waiting to greet me accompanied by a lady
who was literally waving her cheque book in my direction. She
was all set to write a cheque for the extremely modest sum I
was asking; what she wanted was a static houseboat for herself
and her elderly father. I had a clear conscience about such a
sale because I knew that despite *Cressy*'s inward rottenness she
was perfectly capable of staying afloat for years. But when
Wyatt insisted on a hull survey in the dry dock at Stone before
any money passed, I knew at once that this amounted to sentence
of death. Sure enough, a boatbuilder from the Anderton
Company unhesitatingly condemned her. I spent a few more
melancholy days on board sorting out and packing my portable
belongings to be sent home. Most of *Cressy*'s equipment consisted of fixtures that were still as sound and serviceable as on
the day they were made, yet were doomed to die with her. I
thought of all the satisfaction, the energy and the optimism that

I had put into their designing and making just twelve years before. Mel, who had volunteered to drive me back to my mother's house in Gloucestershire, drove on to the Wharf. I heard the crunching sound of the tyres and knew that the moment had come. I glanced around; at the bunches of bright painted roses on the wall panels of our stateroom and on both sets of cabin doors; at the painted castle in the forecabin, at the scratch-comb graining and at the brave chequerwork of the leg of our folding dining table. Then I shut the cabin doors behind me and turned my back on her for the last time. I did not look back as we drove away. From now on I should be living 'on the bank' as the canal boaters put it.

I understand that *Cressy* lay at Stone Wharf for some weeks, if not months, before they towed her away to some backwater of the Trent & Mersey where they left her to sink and rot. I have never inquired the precise whereabouts of this watery grave because I did not want to see her again. Yet for over twenty years, from her birth as a houseboat on the Welsh Border to her death at Stone, the old boat had exercised far too important an influence over my life to be banished from my mind. There could be no forgetting, and for years after I used frequently to dream that I was back on board. Often it was in circumstances of dire emergency like drifting out of control towards a weir on a rapid current. Maybe this was the psychological price to be paid for the many hazards I had managed to avoid either by luck or judgement during my boating years.

Not since the failure of Kerr Stuarts in 1930, which I described in the first volume of this autobiography, had I felt so disorientated, not to say disenchanted, as I did during the few weeks I spent with my mother at Stanley Pontlarge after abandoning *Cressy*. Once again I had built around myself what I believed to be a stable world but now the whole fabric seemed to have crumbled about my ears; my marriage had broken, my home was gone and the canal crusade to which I had devoted so much energy, time and enthusiasm had ended in futile and degrading bickering. In short, I felt very sorry for myself at this moment. Even the fact that six books of mine had been published since the appearance of *Narrow Boat* seemed small consolation. For although these books received

187

good notices and, in fact, two of them, like *Narrow Boat*, are still in print today, in my gloomy mood I had become convinced that so far as the reading public was concerned I was a 'one-book' author.

However, the support of staunch friends was something I had not had at the previous débâcle in my life. I shall always remember Gunde Griffith's vigorous refutation when, wallowing in an ecstasy of self-pity, I declared that the whole of my twelve years with Angela on *Cressy* had been a disastrous and unproductive failure. This, she replied tartly, was utter nonsense and I should know better. The present cannot undo the past, she pointed out. Nothing which had endured for twelve years could conceivably be judged a failure, and in fact the whole long episode of living afloat had been an immensely rewarding and creative experience for us both. Now, like all good things, it had come to an end. Instead of bewailing and belittling what had gone, I should have the grace to be thankful for past favours and the courage to turn the page and begin another chapter. Fortunately, and quite fortuitously, the means were at hand to enable me to do just this.

Over the special meeting of the I.W.A. in Birmingham which broke my last link with the canals, it were best to draw a kindly veil. Squabbles of this kind which seem so momentous when they take place, stand revealed by the passage of time as the trivial things they really are. They bring out all that is worst in human nature, and this goes for both sides and does not exclude myself. Suffice it to say that the 'heretics' lost the day by a narrow margin, leaving the opposing caucus triumphant in the stricken field. I left the hall with a decidedly unpleasant taste in my mouth and, by one of those strange coincidences which sometimes occur in life, walked into another and much pleasanter meeting held in a small office in Waterloo Street, Birmingham, a mere three hundred yards away. This was one of the first – if not the first – committee meetings of the recently formed Talyllyn Railway Preservation Society. But how this swift transition from canal to rail came about is another story.